£12·75

Manufacturing
in the Backyard

Manufacturing in the Backyard

Case Studies on Accumulation and Employment in Small-scale Brazilian Industry

Hubert Schmitz

Frances Pinter (Publishers), London

Allanheld, Osmun Publishers, New Jersey

First published in Great Britain in 1982 by
Frances Pinter (Publishers) Limited
5 Dryden Street, London WC2E 9NW

ISBN 0 86187 230 4

Published in the United States of America in 1982
by Allanheld, Osmun & Co. Publishers, Inc.
(A Division of Littlefield, Adams and Company)
81 Adams Drive, Totowa, New Jersey 07512

Library of Congress Cataloging in Publication Data

Schmitz, Hubert
    Manufacturing in the Backyard

    Bibliography: P.
    includes index
    1. Small Business — Brazil — Case Studies.
    2. Under-developed Areas — Small Business — Case Studies
I. Title
HD2346.B7S34   338.6′42′0981   81-17604
ISBN 0-86598-076-4 (Allanheld, Osmun) AACR2

Printed in Great Britain by
Redwood Burn Ltd., Trowbridge, Wiltshire.

For Suzanne

TABLE OF CONTENTS

LIST OF TABLES

ACKNOWLEDGEMENTS

This study has benefited from the help of many people. By far the greatest debt is to Manfred Bienefeld who supervised the research at the stage of its conception and during writing up. In the course of many discussions he guided me through the extensive debate on industrialisation and employment; his detailed and incisive comments on previous drafts helped to clarify the arguments; his encouragement and generous advice made it a pleasure to work together.

The collection of information was carried out during an assignment to the UNDP/ILO Human Resources Planning Project in Brazil. I wish to thank its director Samuel Levy for giving me the opportunity to combine advisory work with these research activities and Líscio Fabio do Brasil Camargo for his support in the fieldwork. My thanks also go to all the respondents, who gave me many valuable hours of their time during interviews, discussions and visits to their places of work.

At various stages of the research I gratefully received support and helpful criticisms from Antonio Cabral de Andrade, José Eduardo Cassiolato, José Olímpio Coelho, Charles Cooper, Paulo Vieira da Cunha, Pedro Demo, Fabio Erber, Douglas Hindson, George Martine, Anna Luiza Ozorio de Almeida, José Carlos Peliano, Claudio Salm, and Hans Singer.

Finally a special 'thank you' to Suzanne Perfrement for many valuable discussions throughout the work and for help in turning a clumsy manuscript into a readable text.

Of course none of the above can be held responsible for any errors in this study.

INTRODUCTION

The role of small enterprises in providing earning opportunities has been one of the central concerns in the recent debate on urban employment problems in developing countries. By the beginning of the seventies it was generally recognised that, despite high rates of economic growth, most developing economies had been unable to productively employ and adequately remunerate the available labour force. Hopes that rapid growth of the modern industrial sector could solve the problems of underemployment and poverty were not fulfilled. It was found that a considerable part of the urban population made its living in small-scale activities about which very little was known. Many of these activities were not officially registered and escaped statistical surveys. Not surprisingly, subsequent research on this part of the economy proved to be difficult, but shed some light on what came to be called the 'urban traditional sector', 'informal sector', 'marginal pole', or 'lower circuit' of the economy.

The conclusions reached on the actual or potential role of these small-scale activities in providing employment and income differ widely. In some cases these differences reflect different realities, in others they are more a result of the different approaches of the researchers. In the study that follows, an attempt is made to review the available evidence and present some new material drawn from a number of case studies. To this end we will investigate two questions:

- how viable were the small-scale producers in the situations examined and what growth constraints were they up against?

- what employment and income conditions arose from these constraints and how did these conditions compare with those of workers in larger enterprises?

Throughout, the discussion will concentrate on urban small-scale manufacturing and the focus will be on enterprises of

1

up to ten workers.

The work is divided into three parts. <u>Part 1</u> reviews the literature. It begins with the issue of whether small-scale producers in developing countries can expand or whether they are up against constraints which stunt their growth. Most of the literature has been optimistic on this score; while internal constraints (e.g. lack of managerial ability) or external constraints (e.g. discrimination from government) are identified, expansion is seen as an open-ended process. In other contributions this view has been severely criticised; some allege that the small producers are exploited through various mechanisms, others suggest that their road to expansion is blocked as a result of factors such as the pre-existence of very advanced technology, the control of large firms over product markets, or difficulties in access to raw materials. In discussing the arguments put forward in that debate, an attempt is made to assess their theoretical bases and examine the extent to which they are supported empirically. While most studies express (explicity or implicity) a definite view on the growth potential of small producers, such judgement is rarely based on a comprehensive examination of the context which determines this potential.

The concern with the growth constraints of small-scale activities is ultimately derived from our interest in the earning opportunities they provide. The second section of Part 1 reviews how the earnings in the small-scale sector compare with those of wage workers in larger enterprises. Some studies suggest that those engaged in small-scale activities are generally unable to find a job in larger enterprises and form the bulk of the urban poor, whereas those employed in larger enterprises are relatively privileged. Other studies challenge this view, alleging that small-scale producers are better off and do not aspire to wage employment in larger enterprises. In reviewing the available evidence it is shown how the differences in findings can partly be explained by the definitions used and the degree of differentiation between activities and between heads of small enterprises and their workers.

In <u>Part 2</u> these issues are examined on the basis of

three case studies carried out in Brazil. The research approach adopted for these case studies rests on three premises: .

-   while our ultimate concern is the employment and income of people, the unit of analysis should be the enterprise whose condition of operation determines the availability and terms of work;

-   at our present state of knowledge we cannot sensibly investigate these conditions of operation for the small-scale sector as a whole, and the most fruitful way of proceeding is through research by branch activity;

-   these branch studies should include both small and large enterprises, as the relationships between them are likely to be crucial determinants of the conditions of production and employment in the small enterprises.

In the course of the fieldwork we discovered that many of the small manufacturers were in fact clandestine, often operating from their own backyards or those of other domestic premises. The first case study was carried out in the knitting and clothing industry of Petrópolis, state of Rio de Janeiro. Most small enterprises in this industry were set up by former skilled employees of larger enterprises in an attempt to improve their economic and social situation. The technological conditions in this industry open up this route of mobility, but at the same time allow for intensive competition, where survival and expansion require increased work hours or the inclusion of family labour. While most small producers manage to earn more than wage workers, accumulation is very difficult and some of the external obstacles emphasised in the literature are real. Nevertheless some small producers manage to grow and find room in the market, because their flexibility is greater than that of large firms. This is essential in knitted clothing, the demand for which is very volatile due to changing fashions and seasons and channelled through a very diffuse distribution network. For the same reason the conditions of production and income are unstable.

The second case study deals with the hammock industry of Fortaleza in the North East. Technology in the hammock industry has virtually stagnated and most operations are still manual. Given the limits of mechanisation employers' main strategy has been to lower labour costs by registering only part of the internal workforce, subcontracting small non-registered domestic workshops which rely on family labour, and extensive use of outworkers. Some small producers manage to produce and sell independently (i.e. are not subcontracted), but competition is fierce, limiting the profits of all small producers. Even though they earn more than wage workers, it is difficult for them to accumulate sufficiently in order to expand. Workshops are not threatened by technological change, but their production and income are very unstable due to factors outside their control. Their main problem is the supply of raw material whose availability and price are manipulated by big spinning companies and the Government.

Small producers in the third case study, the weaving industry of Americana in the state of São Paulo, are virtually all subcontracted. Many of the large enterprises owe their growth to the use of such external subcontracted workshops, which are generally set up by skilled workers. However, this movement from wage employment to subcontractor is gradually coming to an end, because technological change has increased the entry barriers. Existing subcontractors operate under conditions of severe competition and suffer from the instability of orders from the parent firms. Indeed the small producers feel the brunt of fluctuations in the market, causing a high turnover amongst them. While many still manage to do better than they would as employees, there is little question that subcontracting and with it the importance of small producers is declining.

The case studies are preceded by a brief review of the recent performance of the Brazilian economy and a survey of the development of production and employment in the three industries investigated, all based on secondary sources. The case studies themselves are almost entirely based on our own information and the main objective of Part 2 is to present the findings of the field work.

In <u>Part 3</u> some wider implications of the case studies are examined in relation to the two main issues raised in Part 1, that of employment and income and that of growth constraints. The case studies reveal very clearly that small producers are <u>not</u> unsuccessful job seekers but relatively skilled workers who left their jobs of their own accord. They find that setting up their own business gives them a better chance for economic and social advance than wage employment. Obviously this route is not open for all workers, but it is a significant factor in explaining the emergence of small enterprises.

The main reason for leaving a job seems to be the low wages; other reasons are connected with the desire to be more 'independent'; but the aspiration to 'independence' is often an illusion, because by escaping factory work, many do not entirely escape wage work: in a subcontracting relationship their small workshop is merely an extension of the parent firm's factory in which they, the owners, are disguised workers, or supervisors (if they have wage workers themselves), who are paid a 'premium' in boom periods and abandoned in times of recession. However, such working arrangements are seen by the respondents as a gateway to setting up as an independent producer, that is buying one's own raw material and marketing one's own product. The route is clearly a risky one but apparently worth taking because even as small subcontractors they generally manage to earn more than factory workers. However, as is stressed throughout the work, such comparisons are problematic due to the involvement of family labour in small enterprises. The conditions of non-family wage workers in these enterprises vary, but they tend to have the lowest remuneration of all categories of labour considered.

In terms of growth constraints, the research suggests that problems internal to the small enterprises can hardly be regarded as major obstacles to their expansion. This does not mean that there are no internal problems in particular cases, but the case studies give little reason to support those who see lack of entrepreneurship, management and skills as general retarding factors. Small enterprises often give the appearance of organisational chaos due to their need for flexibility and improvisation and due to the integration of family and business, but their internal characteristics can be a source of strength, especially in times of crises.

External constraints are identified in the case studies, in particular problems of access to raw materials. These force many small producers into a subcontracting relationship with larger enterprises, which in turn makes it difficult for them to retain the surplus produced; a comparison in one of the case studies suggests that independent small producers earn twice as much. However, the main problem of small enterprises that are stuck in subcontracting or similar arrangements is the irregularity of work. In one of the branches, technological discontinuities are also threatening the small-scale producers, even though these can be somewhat reduced through the use of second-hand machinery. The expansion of small producers in general is further hampered by government policies. Concrete policy implications are discussed for the branches examined, but the introduction of such measures is thought to be unlikely because the pursued policies are an outcome of the well entrenched access to the state machinery which large-scale capital maintains.

In spite of the severe difficulties found in the small producers' struggle for survival or expansion, the case studies do not entirely support a theory of marginalisation as the general paradigm of small-scale producers in developing countries. The pressures emphasised by those who put forward this view are real, but the conditions which determine their strength vary and must be specified. Therefore the issue should not be whether small enterprises have growth and employment potential but under what conditions.

Caution is necessary in drawing conclusions from such a small number of case studies, but it is believed that this detailed investigation of a limited number of activities provides some insights which escape most large-scale surveys aiming at statistically generalisable findings. In a methodological section at the end of Part 3 the advantages and limitations of both approaches are discussed. Relatively large-scale cross-section surveys in selected cities of developing countries are the most widely used method in recent reseach. Given that the world of small producers is in most cases an uncharted territory, such surveys are useful in filling the gap left by official establishment surveys. However, they tend to fall down badly on the question of growth constraints, even though this is the use to which they are often put. Pre-coded questionnaires applied across all branches of activity are unsuitable instruments for unravelling the circumstances which determine the constraints or opportunities of small producers. It is argued that detailed branch-specific studies are the most useful way of getting a grip on these factors and that such studies should not only cover the small producers themselves but also related large producers and suppliers of raw material and technology. Furthermore, approaching these producers and suppliers not just as 'sources of data' but as 'informants on what is going on in the industry' is essential to gain a better understanding of the context in which the small producers operate. This method is of great help especially in research where, for practical reasons, the size of the sample has to be kept small and where the sampling universe is not known.

In summary, our major concern is to understand the functioning of the industry in order to understand the problems of production and employment in the small enterprises within it. This is believed to be the major contribution to the general analysis of small-scale manufacturing in developing countries. However, at the end of this work the question is raised of whether this context is defined widely enough and whether it sufficiently encompasses changes in the national and global economy.

PART 1

GROWTH CONSTRAINTS AND EARNING OPPORT-UNITIES IN SMALL-SCALE MANUFACTURING OF DEVELOPING COUNTRIES

The most influential force in placing urban small producers at the centre of the recent employment debate was the Report of the ILO Kenya Mission (ILO, 1972). The report's message was very clear: approximately one-third of the African urban population earns its living in activities which are characterised by 'ease of entry, reliance on indigenous resources, family ownership of enterprises, small scale of operation, labour-intensive and adapted technology, skills acquired outside the formal school system, and unregulated and competitive markets' (p. 6). These activities, according to the mission, far from being stagnant and only marginally productive, form a sector of thriving economic activity which has the potential for dynamic, evolutionary growth.

Clearly this report was not just a piece of research but an explicitly political document; the mission's insistence on the dynamism and potential of the above mentioned sector came less from empirical evidence than from the need to draw the attention of politicians, planners and administrators to a neglected but important part of the urban economy. It did so by giving these activities the label of the 'informal sector',[1] by putting forward the view of this sector as a source of future growth and productive employment, and by recommending that the government stop discriminating against these activities; rather it should actively support them by channelling more resources into the informal sector and forging more links between it and the formal sector.

This was both a challenging and useful step to take; challenging because dependency theory was rapidly gaining ground at the time, questioning whether capitalism could play a progressive role in the development of the indigenous productive forces of less developed countries (Frank, 1971); useful because, as pointed out by Bienefeld and Godfrey (1975), the employment debate had become preoccupied with <u>measuring</u> the underutilisation of labour

9

and had drifted into futile discussions about which criteria should be used to classify people as employed, underemployed and unemployed. The ILO Kenya report rightly rejected these exercises and focussed attention on the more important issue of what people actually do if they are not directly employed in the formal sector, what potential their activities have, and what income they can derive from them.

In the wake of the ILO's official endorsement of the informal sector concept, there was a worldwide upsurge in research on urban small-scale activities. Since the concept was used by different people for different purposes, no attempt will be made here to trace all the directions which the discussion took. Bromley (1978a) has pointed to the forces which explain the rapid acceptance of the term 'informal sector' in the 'international academic and policy-prescribing network' (p. 1036); a number of reviews has traced the ideological and intellectual history of the formal-informal sector distinction and put some order into the rather confused debate (Bienefeld and Godfrey, 1975, 1978; Breman, 1976; Moser, 1978; Nihan, 1979; Tokman, 1978; Raczynski, 1977; Senghaas-Knobloch, 1978; Villavicencio, 1976).

This recent debate on the informal sector will only be referred to where it has a direct bearing on the issues raised in this work. The objective of this first part is to review what the literature in general has to say on growth constraints and earning opportunities in urban small-scale manufacturing[2] of developing countries. Most of the literature referred to deals with enterprises of between one and ten workers, but in a few cases it includes enterprises of a somewhat larger scale. The terminology used varies and includes among others: informal sector, urban traditional sector, lower circuit, marginal pole, unprotected sector, non-enumerated sector, domestic workshops, petty commodity production, non-capitalist (or not-typically capitalist) production. Even though authors sometimes emphasise these terminological distinctions, by and large they refer to the same group of enterprises, at least when considering manufacturing.

1.1 <u>Growth Constraints of Small Enterprises</u>

By most standards, the small industrialists of Chopur (North India) **are good** industrial entrepreneurs. They live frugally and save. They are highly skilled themselves or employ skilled personnel. They are quality-conscious, able to make improvements in technique on their own, quick to learn from others.

As entrepreneurs, they are tenacious to an extreme. When one industrial venture fails, their first act is to begin scraping together savings for another.

As manufacturers they are versatile and resourceful with the few resources at their command. If they cannot buy a machine, they will build it themselves. If they cannot reproduce a technique, they will improvise one of their own. Most are sensitive to new demands and market changes as their information and their circumstances permit.

The small industrialists of Chopur have every earmark of the successful entrepreneur, <u>except success.</u>

By and large, they do not prosper. When they do prosper, it is not for long .... The small industrial firms of Chopur have never grown beyond a certain point, as if there were a physical barrier between the small and medium-size range impossible to cross. (McCrory quoted from Staley and Morse, 1965, p.233)

This quote sets the scene for the discussion in this section. Its author ascribed the failure of small enterprises to breach the size barrier primarily to <u>external</u> problems, in particular to the unavailability of capital from any dependable outside source. Staley and Morse, however, in commenting on this study, raise the question of <u>internal</u> problems and question 'whether lack of capital may not be a symptom in some cases of other handicaps, especially unskilled management and lack of education' (p.233). In

11

general, the growth constraints identified in the literature can be grouped into these two categories: those of an internal nature (entrepreneurship, management) and those of an external nature (access to resources, exploitation by larger enterprises).

Internal Factors: Entrepreneurship and Management

In the literature which emphasises the internal problems, the growth of small producers is seen to be a process which is open-ended but held back by the lack of entrepreneurial or managerial skills. Thus Kilby (1969) writes in an assessment of the Nigerian industrialisation experience:

> What then is the proper development perspective on the small scale industrial sector? As a quasi sponge for urban unemployment and a provider of inexpensive consumer goods with little or no import content, this sector serves important pressure-releasing, welfare-augmenting functions. Its more positive role in contributing to long run industrial growth is to produce an increasing number of firms that grow up and out of the small-scale sector. The emergence of wholly modern, medium-scale Nigerian industry is likely to be a prerequisite for any enduring industrialisation. As we shall see subsequently, the problems encountered in attempting to develop the most promising firms are ultimately related to questions of entrepreneurship. (p.310)

Kilby furthermore suggests that these are part of a deeper problem:

> The roots of entrepreneurial deficiencies ... may run deeper than the mere lack of experience and training. The underlying attitudes and dispositions of entrepreneurs ... would seem to a considerable degree to be

independent of the level of education or training .... In brief, what is being suggested here is that the development of certain requisite entrepreneurial characteristics, relating to performance in the organisational and technological spheres, is being impeded by traditional socio-cultural factors common to all of Nigeria's ethnic groups. (p.341)

Leaving aside the dubious 'ethnic' question, no serious economist would deny the importance of entrepreneurship in industrialisation,[3] but the issue is whether we can explain the lack of thriving small-scale industry by a lack of the 'right' entrepreneurial attitudes.

Stepanek (1960) also regards the lack of entrepreneurial and managerial ability as the major bottleneck. He draws this conclusion from several years of work as senior advisor for small-scale industrial development in Asia.[4] One wonders however about the soundness of this judgement when one reads that 'the only way to measure the development of an entrepreneur-manager is to observe what happens to the enterprise. If it is successful, we can assume that the manager has developed' (p.7)! This quote reveals the frequently tautological nature of explanations based on lack of entrepreneurship or management.

The concern with management reappears in a more recent study on 'the modern informal sector in Lomé', Togo, which concludes that

> the main problem facing the informal sector arises out of its very rough and ready methods of enterprise management and price fixing. The standards of technical management and book-keeping are pretty poor whatever the level of capital investment. (Nihan, Demol and Jondoh, 1979, p.635)

Quantitative evidence is then provided to illustrate the poor standards. While this information is useful, it is not clear what enables the authors to turn the findings on this question into conclusions about the major bottleneck. Again, what is at issue is not that good management is important, but whether small–scale producers in developing countries fail to expand primarily because they lack managerial ability.

A detailed analysis would probably have to distinguish between questions related to (a) motivation, drive, adaptability, (b) organisational skills, and (c) technical skills. Most detailed descriptions of the urban small–scale economy in less developed countries would certainly defy the first concern. They tend to reveal great initiative, inventiveness, responsiveness and readiness to jump at opportunities (Hart, 1973; King, 1974; Peattie, 1978). On the question of organisational deficiencies, one wonders to what extent this concern stems from having identified this as a real problem in small enterprises or from the analysts' backgrounds in management studies. In many cases there is a severe limit to advance planning and organisation in small enterprises, as a result of the market in which they operate or a shortage of resources. Their survival and growth often require above all flexibility and ability to improvise, which might give the external observer an impression of chaos. The appearance of messiness might be further aggravated if the small enterprise is run on a family basis; this means on the negative side intrusion of family problems, usually outweighed on the positive side by little need for internal paper work and formal organisation. Finally on the question of technical skills we can tread on firmer ground due to King's work (1974, 1975, 1979). He studied questions of technical skills and training in East Africa, where they could be expected to represent a particularly severe problem because of a comparative lack of traditional skill specialisation and formalised apprenticeship in that area. Yet his conclusion on the obstacles confronting the small producer is that

> there are presently severe structural problems restricting his development into an own-account worker capable of the production of high quality precision goods. It is not principally the technical dimension which

constitutes the obstacle, but rather the lack of a basic credit infrastructure, security of tenure in the urban areas, and a technology policy that would support the very small-scale entrepreneur. (1979, p.228, emphasis added)

External Factors

Let us turn to these 'structural' or 'external' factors. The arguments in the literature which emphasise their importance fall into two groups: one group suggests that the small producers are exploited by the large firms through various mechanisms and thus contribute to the accumulation of capital in those large enterprises. In a second set of arguments the road to expansion is considered to be blocked for the small producers as a result of difficulties in access to product markets, technology, raw material or credit; government policies are seen as reinforcing these blockages. Some authors suggest that they are so severe that the growth of small producers is stunted or can only be involutionary; others acknowledge the existence of these blockages but suggest that they can be removed or leave enough room for evolutionary growth. Let us examine the arguments in detail.

The 'exploitation approach' is exemplified in Leys' critique of the ILO Kenya Mission's recommendations to effect closer links between the informal and formal sectors.

What the "informal sector" does is to provide the "formal sector" with goods and services at very low prices, which makes possible the high profits of the "formal sector." Smallholders provide cheap food crops, pastoralists cheap beef, traders cheap distribution, transporters cheap communications; the owners of workshops making shoes out of old tyres and stoves out of old tins, the sellers of charcoal and millers of maize; all of them provide cheap goods and services designed for the poverty life style of those whose work makes the "formal sector" profitable, and enables them to live on their wages. (Leys, 1975, pp.267–8, emphasis added)

The Cheap Wage Goods Issue

The examples given by Leys imply that the urban petty producers help to keep the price of labour power low, and thus contribute to an increase in surplus value and the accumulation of capital in industry. Similar arguments have been put forward with regard to the role of subsistence agriculture and also urban domestic production for the cheapening of the costs of reproduction of the industrial labour force (Meillassoux, 1972; Wolpe, 1972; Gardiner, 1975; Woortman, 1980). The theoretical issues involved are very complex, and cannot be adequately dealt with here, let alone resolved. However, the significance of the argument should be assessed for the case of urban petty production of marketed wage goods. According to Portes (1978),

> the fundamental point is that the informal sector subsidizes part of the costs of formal capitalist enterprises in peripheral capitalist countries, enabling them to reinforce comparatively low wages on their own labour. The basic needs of formal sector workers are partially met by goods and services produced using unpaid or more cheaply paid informal labour. (p.37, emphasis added)

Even though this argument keeps surfacing in the more radical literature on urban poverty, it has to our knowledge rarely, if ever, been subjected to detailed empirical examination.[5] Presumably such an investigation would have to begin with a list of the material needs of an industrial worker and his family, and examine how these needs were satisfied (or possibly not satisfied) and where the required goods and services came from. Casual observation would suggest that there is a significant difference between, for example, African and South American countries. In

Nairobi,

> the urban informal sector produces the following range of goods and services. In manufacturing, wearing apparel, footwear, furniture and metal goods are the dominant sectors and satisfy the basic demands of the poor for clothes, shoes and household durable goods such as tables, chairs, beds, charcoal, braziers (jikos), cooking pots (sufurias), etc. Many carpenters appear to be engaged in the construction sector, building low cost wooden houses in the so-called "slum" areas of Nairobi ... (Ghai, Godfrey, Lisk, 1979, p.116)

In São Paulo or Rio de Janeiro this would not be so, as most of these goods are produced in capitalist enterprises. Indeed the greater part of the worker's family budget is spent on industrialised goods (P.Singer, 1977).[6] According to Webb (1974) three-quarters of the expenditure of urban low-income families in Peru went on products from the 'modern sector'.

From this point of view it is somewhat surprising that the 'cheap wage goods issue' is relatively little discussed in the literature on urban small producers in Africa, but figures very prominently in the Latin American literature, most notably in the Brazilian debate. Following the reasoning of Oliveira (1972), Kowarick in his book, Capitalism and Marginality in Latin America (1975), suggests that those activities considered 'marginal', when 'producing commodities as artisans or in small domestic enterprises, or selling services and goods of all types ... lower the costs of reproduction of the urban labour force' (p.84). '... their insertion in the productive system constitutes types of exploitation different from those characteristic of the "integrated" working class...' (p.85). Prandi (1978) takes up this point and makes it the central argument of a study on the self-employed in Brazil. He distinguishes between those involved in manufacturing, repairs, trade, services and transport, but for the self-employed as a whole (with the exception of the professions)

17

he comes to the conclusion that the logic of their existence lies in lowering the costs of reproduction of labour, and that they are increasingly left with low-income markets which in turn lowers their own remuneration (p.138).

There would seem to be a number of problems with this position: first, there is the empirical question already mentioned, since, at least in Brazil, the non-agricultural wage goods come in the main from the capitalist sector. As for the question of the self-employed being geared increasingly towards the low-income population, this is neither convincingly supported by Prandi's own data nor by other Brazilian studies.[7]

Second, if the 'subsidy' is thought to be due to extra low levels of remuneration of petty producers, one needs to know why this remuneration is so low. If it is forced on them by the greater efficiency of expanding capitalist production, then clearly there is no subsidy; the remuneration is low because productivity is lower than that of competitors, or in other words, because the amount of labour time is higher than socially necessary. Under such circumstances the acceptance of ever lower incomes can, for a time, compensate for this productivity difference, but eventually the small-scale producers will be forced out of that line of production.

Third, if it is extreme competition amongst petty producers which forces them to use unpaid family labour or underpaid wage labour (e.g. in the form of apprentices) then indeed mechanisms must be at work which prevent the petty producers reaping the benefits of their labour and accumulating the surplus. Thus, the intense competition may enable the buyers of their products to channel the surplus away from the small-scale sector, especially if competition among the buyers themselves is reduced. However, the loss of this surplus for the small producers does not necessarily result in cheaper wage goods for the worker. It is possible that the buyers (intermediaries) retain that surplus. Therefore, at least as far as the question of the growth potential of small producers is concerned, it would seem more useful (a) to focus more on the question of whether the small producers can retain the surplus and (b) to separate this question from that of the

18

costs of reproduction of the urban industrial labour force. In the context of our discussion we are mainly concerned with (a) and we shall return to it later.

A comment should, however, be made on the question of whether the maintenance of small-scale wage goods production is functional for the process of capitalist expansion. Portes (1978) categorically asserts this functionality, when he states that capitalism is 'dependent on the informal sector' (p.35). It would seem that such a formulation turns the theory of capitalist accumulation on its head by positing a dependency on that part of the economy which is the least developed. In discussing the functionality, it is probably more adequate to put it in the context of the <u>disruptive</u> nature of the process of industrialisation in the periphery. Because of this, a subsistence base not entirely dependent on wage employment in the capitalist sector can indeed be vital to absorb and defuse the general fluctuations in wage employment and income, particularly when social services and social security provisions are absent. Under such circumstances the employers or the state are spared the costs of these services,[8] and could therefore have an interest in conserving the non-capitalist production.[9] This, however, only persists until the direct employment of this labour force in capitalist enterprises becomes a possibility and promises gains which outweigh the costs of alternative social security provisions (Bienefeld and Schmitz, 1976).

Direct Production for Large Firms

Other critiques of the optimistic view of the development potential of small firms stipulate a much more direct relationship of dependence and exploitation between the petty producer and the capitalist sector in the form of the subcontracting or putting out system.

Subcontracting seems to be most widely practised in the construction industry. In Dakar, for instance,

> in certain activities such as concrete-reinforcing, tiling, painting and bricklaying the construction companies, rather than engage

wage workers, employ tâcherons. These are petty producers who do piece and contract-work for industrial capital using their own journeymen and apprentices as labourers. The labourers receive very low remuneration, and the system permits the construction enterprises to lower their production costs, since there is virtually nothing to pay for the labour-power obtained, no pension schemes or social benefits of any kind to which they must contribute. (Le Brun and Gerry, 1975, pp.27-8)

A similar set-up is known for the construction industry in other countries (e.g. Scott, 1979; Stretton, 1979), including Britain, where it is known by the unlovely term of the 'lump'. We shall not however follow up these cases, as we are more concerned here with the manufacturing sector.

Scott (1979) observed that in Lima self-employed manufacturers found it increasingly difficult to survive as independent producers and became out-workers or subcontractors.

(Subcontracting) is commonest in the footwear and clothing industry, although it has also been found in such unexpected branches of production as the manufacture of refrigerators, transport vehicles, and stationery products. Out-workers may be contracted by commercial or industrial firms .... The existence of this putting out system leads to a chain of subcontracting between out-workers. For example, one tailor was able to run a small workshop with eight wage labourers on the basis of outwork contracts from merchant capit-alists. Another example was a cobbler who was making shoes for a small workshop which was itself subcontracted to the multi-national firm, Bata. (p.114)

Bose (1978) in his study on the slum industries of

Calcutta states that 'the existence of the large houses controlling the market ensures effectively that the informal sector producers will have to hand over their produce to the organised sector for marketing the goods they themselves have produced' (p.98). His examples include small family-based footwear manufacturers and small-scale units in mechanical or electrical engineering, which produce at very low prices parts or complete products for large firms which sell them at high profits. He concludes that in 'this relationship of what may be called exploitation between the large and small units, the latter can exist, given the present socio-economic structure, only when they can get the opportunity of offering themselves to be "exploited" by the larger units' (p.105).

An examination of this issue is indeed highly important because ultimately one needs to know to what extent the small producers are independent or simply an extension of the production network of large firms, a sort of disguised wage labour. If the latter is the case, one would like to know whether this practice tends to be replaced by direct employment in large firms or whether it serves as an entry point for small producers to expand and eventually become independent. These questions are but little examined for developing countries, the most pertinent literature dealing with the advanced countries and their history.

Marx (1970, 1971) and Dobb (1975) analysed the role of the putting out system in the industrialisation of Britain and Western Europe and saw it very much as a transitory form which was soon to make room for the direct subordination of labour in capitalist production. This view can also be found in Lenin's writings (1977a, 1977b). He examined the question in great detail because in the 1890s there was an extensive discussion in his country about whether and how the small producers should be supported.

Lenin's (1977a) main point is that large parts of what are called 'handicraft industries' are extensions or departments of capitalist manufacture. Indeed his main critique of a census of small-scale producers is that with all the richness of the information that the census provides, it obscures the essential fact of small-scale industry 'performing nothing but detailed operations in the

21

large-scale capitalist manufacture' (p.427) or producing complete products for merchant capital (p.424).

> It would not be amiss to make a detailed study of its actual organisation, a study of the conditions which make it preferable for manufacturers to give out work to be done in the home. The manufacturers undoubtedly find it more profitable, and we shall understand why if we bear in mind the low earnings of the handicraft men in general .... By giving out material to be worked up at home, the employers lower wages, economise on premises, partly on implements, and on supervision, ... get workers who are more scattered, disunited, and less capable of self defence, and also unpaid task masters for these workers ... in the shape of those handicraftsmen they employ and who, in their turn, employ wage-workers ... these wage-workers receive the lowest wages of all. And this is not surprising, for they are subjected to double exploitation: exploitation by their own employer who squeezes his "own little profit" out of the workers, and exploitation by the manufacturer who gives out material to the small masters. We know that these small middlemen, who are well familiar with local conditions and with the personal characteristics of the workers, are particularly prolific in inventing different forms of extortion ... (p.428)

In the course of a very detailed critique of the methods and concepts used in the collection, processing and analysis of the census data, Lenin launches a vigorous attack on those 'petty bourgeois theorists' who devise policies for the support of small-scale producers. In his view, such measures would, first, mainly benefit the buyer-up (parent firm); second, help to preserve conditions of work and remuneration far worse than those of the workers directly employed by capitalist firms; and third, retard the development of industry and fully fledged capitalism. 'The Narodniks contrive to cling to their intention of <u>retarding</u> contemporary economic development, of <u>preventing</u> the progress of capitalism, and of <u>supporting</u> small production, which is being bled white in the struggle against large-scale production' (p.448).

This was written in 1897, in an article, 'The Handicraft Census of 1894–95 in Perm Gubernia and General Problems of "Handicraft" Industry'. Even though the article is part of a polemic against the Narodniks, it is very pertinent for the current informal sector discussion, because there are compelling parallels between the latter and the Russian discussion on handicraft industry; for example, Lenin illustrates very clearly the pitfalls of analysing the small-scale producers on the basis of cross-section data, divorced from a general understanding of the industrial structure in which they operate.[10]

However, there are some difficulties with Lenin's view on the long-run tendencies. First, why should support for small-scale producers retard industrialisation, if they are shown to accelerate accumulation? This seems to be a conflict in his argument. Second, it is true that large-scale operation with the <u>direct</u> employment of labour has progressively taken over branches which were formerly characterised by the putting out system. But this process has been very uneven, as pointed out by Schmukler (1977) in a study which stresses the heterogeneity of forms of production found in Argentinian industry. She concludes that in some branches the subcontracting of small firms and employment of outworkers 'do not constitute transitional forms towards more mature capitalist relations of production nor do they become an obstacle to the development of capitalism in the branch' (p.16).[11] One should add that in the wake of technological development, conditions for small-scale production and for sub-contracting are continuously recreated. The latest example is the introduction of microelectronics in many branches of manufacturing as a consequence of which the optimal scale of output may be lowered significantly (Kaplinsky, 1979b); it is conceivable that the increased possibilities of small-scale production lead to an increase in subcontracting.

23

Lenin's suggestion that the subcontracting of small producers becomes anachronistic is most clearly belied by the Japanese experience.[12] In Japan, small enterprises and industrial subcontracting have played and are still playing an important role in the economy's rapid industrialisation. Watanabe (1971) stresses that what is peculiar to Japanese manufacturing is not only the great extent of subcontracting but even more 'the efficient use of small enterprises in a wide range of modern industries through subcontracting' (p.52).

A different question is whether those small producers who are subcontracted are able to grow or whether their surplus is syphoned off by the parent firms. In Watanabe's view 'subcontracting can lessen the obstacles to small entrepreneurs setting up in business and can help them, once they are established, to survive and flourish' (1971, p.71). He does not deny the problems that can arise in a subcontracting relationship, but believes nevertheless that it enables a significant number of small producers to accumulate sufficient capital and know-how in order to expand and increase their labour demand. 'Subcontracting can smooth the path of small enterprises and make them a suitable instrument for mass employment creation in developing countries that are committed to industrialisation' (1971, p.51). In a later paper (1978) he stresses the importance of the transfer of technology and know-how from the large to the small producers, as an argument in favour of subcontracting. However, these views are entirely based on the Japanese experience and further research will have to show their relevance for developing countries. Watanabe's own most recent research (1979) in the Philippines shows severe limitation in applying the 'Japanese model'.[13]

Otherwise very little is known about the growth potential of small subcontractors in less developed countries. There is not even a clear picture of the extent of their existence. Tokman (1978) in a review article on the relationships between the formal and informal sectors, concludes that subcontracting is not very important and is concentrated in the clothing industry. Clothing production is indeed a prime example of subcontracting and outwork worldwide (Schmukler, 1977; Hope, Kennedy and de Winter, 1976; Reichmuth, 1978; Sit, Wong and Kiang, 1979), but the question of its significance in other branches of manufacturing in developing countries should be left open. While it seems clear that it is shallow in comparison with Japan (Watanabe, 1978), its real importance remains unknown largely because research on this question is very difficult. Small subcontractors and outworkers are often not registered and therefore do not appear in official statistics. Their true extent and functioning is even difficult to assess in informal sector surveys unless these are combined with detailed branch-specific studies.

Blocked Access

In the discussion of the external growth constraints of small producers one can identify another set of arguments which stress that the small producers' road to expansion is blocked. The blockages are thought to lie in the pre-existence of very advanced technologies and in the control which large firms exercise over product markets, raw materials and credit. This is very much what Quijano (1974) has in mind when he refers to the small producers as the 'marginal pole of the economy', whose defining characteristic is 'the lack of stable access to basic resources of production' (p.404). He sees the main problem in the fact that industrialisation in Latin America did 'not derive from an organic process'; instead a 'hegemonic sector' was 'grafted onto the previous Latin American economic matrix' (p.395). Due to the abrupt incorporation of foreign companies and technologies, the previous activities neither disappear nor properly modernise but are 'modifed by their new modes of articulation in the overall economic structure' and 'occupy an ever more depressed level, due to the continual loss of control of productive resources and markets...' (p.403).

A similar scenario is suggested by Bienefeld (1975) with regard to the East African situation:

... many small scale operators are engaged in a process of production and technological

25

development but their ability to develop cumulatively over extended periods is limited ... by their dependence on large scale industry for inputs (often illegally obtained) and by the fact that when the markets they serve grow beyond a certain size this will not be a gradual ... stimulus to further development of the forces of production. Instead it will trigger a discontinuous shift to "international" technology which will incorporate this market by virtue of its efficiency and/or its market power, the latter based on effectively unlimited access to capital and on the establishment of brand name products through heavy advertising. The net result of this situation is an appearance of virtual stagnation among petty producers, though a more dynamic analysis would possibly reveal a process of growth and destruction. (pp.55-6)

Access to Product Markets

Let us examine these arguments in more detail, beginning with the question of markets. Souza and Tokman in their work on 'The informal urban sector in Latin America' (1976) state that the total market for the sector shows no clear signs of growing.

(The reasons) have to do with the role of small enterprises (in the present case very small ones) in a process of economic growth characterised by the concentration of markets. In highly concentrated oligopolistic markets small enterprises cannot go on increasing the volume of their business indefinitely, and in the long run, despite registering some small temporary gains, they tend to lose markets steadily even if almost imperceptibly. In competitive conditions the informal sector's market grows as a result of rising incomes in that sector or in the economy as a whole, but in most cases its activities are competitive because the size of the market in absolute terms does not yet warrant the establisment of large enterprises. (p.357)

However, as would probably be recognised by the authors themselves, this view cannot be deduced from their extensive empirical work on the informal sector, since their research approach did not lend itself to investigating this process. So what evidence is there that small firms fail to secure or are losing markets?

Bose(1978) in his study on slum industries in Calcutta suggests, on the basis of a number of case studies, that the market for small producers is effectively controlled by large firms; the only way they can gain access to this market is by selling to the large industrial or commercial houses, which sell these products under their brand names, while holding the small producers to ransom through various mechanisms.

Langdon (1975) found in the Kenyan soap industry that small local firms were struggling to survive, despite a growing market for soaps and detergents. Multinational companies had begun to penetrate the market with different products produced with different technologies. Many of the local firms relied on hand methods and had between three and thirty workers; some local firms had begun to mechanise the process. In contrast, the multinational firms moved in with largely automated techniques. The reason for their success, however, lay not in greater efficiency (in terms of providing cheaper and better products to the customer) but in creating a desire for their products through expensive marketing; this included heavy advertising, fancy packaging, different-iation of basically identical products; their production technology also enabled them to give the soap better appearance. Langdon's account is indeed pertinent for our investigation and worth a longer quotation:

the first machine-produced laundry soap in Kenya was mnc produced and that initiative was central in forcing many local firms to

27

mechanise. This impetus was furthered by the mnc advertising campaigns, stressing the general importance of appearance in buying soap - so that by now most hand-production factories cannot sell their output, even at reduced prices, in urban markets in Kenya. This is despite the fact, conceded by some local manufacturers who have mechanised their factories, that hand-processed laundry soap is functionally superior to its machine made equivalent; it has better quality ingredients ... and it lasts longer in cleaning. (p.25)

At a more general level, Langdon concludes,

It would seem there is a similar and pervasive mnc impact on local firms, across a wider range of consumer goods sectors. MNC taste transfer is redefining the basic need for drink into demand for Coke or Pepsi; the basic need for food into demand for Lyon's Maid ice cream or Cadbury's chocolate bars; the basic need for medical aids into demand for Aspro, Cafenol or Cofta; the basic need for baby nourishment into the particularly dangerous demand for Lactogen or Glucorin; the basic need for transport into demand for Peugeots and Mercedes; and so on. Not only do these translations often leave the consumer worse off, paying higher prices to satisfy redefined basic needs. They also, as in the case of soap, generate industrialisation inappropriate to Kenya's resource base and employment needs. And they establish patterns of demand that are very hard for small-scale indigenous Kenyan industrialists to meet directly. In that sense, the mnc role in Kenya seems responsible for blocking, in a general way, the development of decentralised local industry in a wide range of sectors. (p.30, emphasis added)

28

Stewart (1978) reports a similar case for maize grinding in Kenya. Kaplinsky (1979a) in a study on breakfast food in Kenya emphasises that the control of the market is not only exercised by foreign firms, but also by wholly locally-owned firms, albeit producing under licence from foreign suppliers.

Technological Gap

In most of the cases referred to above, the market power of the larger firms is not only based on their marketing strategies but also on their production technology, to which the small producers have no access because it is foreign and/or because initial investment is very high. Bienefeld (1975) suggests that for small enterprises the 'adoption of the latest technology means a <u>discontinuous</u> leap from their previous technology' (p.73, emphasis added). The new technology comes into the developing economy either through foreign firms or a few local firms which receive massive credits from the government or abroad, while the surplus generated in the small-scale sector and the accumulated know-how and skill cannot come into play, hence stunting its growth or even destroying it (pp.72-3). A similar idea is to be found in some of the Latin American dependency literature (e.g. Quijano, 1974) but the technological aspects of such disruptions in local accumulation are not clearly spelt out.

Of course small-scale producers are adversely affected by technical change whenever this leads to increasing economies of scale. This is true for any type of economy, so that the argument does not rest on the adverse effects on small-scale producers caused by technological change as such. It has to rest on some notion of an increasing technological gap which confronts the small producers in the peripheral capitalist countries, and which inhibits continuity in their process of growth. We cannot endeavour here to define such a gap, but it would seem that it has to be seen in a dynamic way and to be related to both the speed or rate at which innovations occur and the location (country, region) in which the capacity to produce innovations develops.

The recent literature on choice of technology in industry, while largely static in its approach, provides some ideas of the jump that is involved in moving from traditional to modern technology. Comparisons of alternative production techniques show enormous differences in initial investment per unit of output or per worker. These studies also reveal that the jump taken is often greater than necessary, because the most modern and expensive technique is not always the economically most efficient for a developing country (Bhalla, 1975). Nevertheless it often displaces the more traditional technique due to a 'more modern is better' mentality. There is now a considerable number of micro case studies confirming these findings (discussed by Stewart, 1978).

On the other hand, the impact which the technologies actually chosen and introduced have had on the development of small-scale producers has been studied surprisingly little. Or perhaps this is not so surprising if one considers that it involves a type of research which is particularly difficult, as the task is one of documenting an historical process. Unless detailed time series data on the number of producers and volume of production exist, these processes are very difficult to reconstruct. This is particularly true if the introduction of new techniques forces small producers into bankruptcy, and even more so, if the effect is one of forestalling local production.

Access to Raw Materials

Difficulties in obtaining raw materials are frequently referred to in the literature on small-scale industry in India. They are said to arise on account of the small producers' bargaining difficulties, their lack of working capital, but also the government's discrimination against small firms in the allocation of raw materials (Dhar and Lydall, 1961; Fisher, 1968; Mars, 1977).

Problems in access to raw materials as a bottleneck for the growth of small producers are particularly emphasised by Gerry (1974, 1978, 1979) in his work on petty production in Dakar, Senegal. He found that in shoe production the small producers had to switch from the use of leather to synthetic materials, since a multinational shoe company was able to achieve a virtual monopsony in the purchase of fine (imported?) leather, and had received considerable government protection. The main importer of synthetic materials then tried to 'reorganise' the small producers using his own capital and marketing outlets, albeit without success.

In more general terms Gerry concludes that 'in an underdeveloped country such as Senegal it is rare to find a productive activity which does not to some extent depend on inputs imported from abroad' (1979, p.232) and that 'in terms of the raw materials ... available to petty producers, the most significant relationship between the latter and the complex of foreign, local or Government controlled industry and commerce is subordination' (p.235). His data, however, show that the degree of 'input-dependency' varies considerably in the four manufacturing branches considered. Eighty per cent of the furniture makers bought their raw materials (imported) from large industrial enterprises. Almost all leather workers purchased raw materials from Mauritanian women who treat and tan hides in traditional manner; but as mentioned above, leather for footwear is being replaced by imported plastic material bought from Lebanese dealers. Some of the metal workers used recycled material purchased from small local dealers while others bought metal from large industrial and commercial firms (1979).[14]

The question is what we make of findings which suggest that in branch X the small producers buy their raw material from a big capitalist enterprise. What significance does this have for their development potential? Gerry tends to equate importation of a raw material or purchase from a large enterprise with dependence or subordination and subsequent inability of the small producer to accumulate. The mechanisms which could produce this stunting effect can be easily envisaged but are not apparent from his work except in the example of shoe production.

Similarly in his first Dakar report (1974), Gerry emphasised the reliance of many petty producers on recycled materials, but the significance of using such inputs is not clear. Does it mean that the supply is unreliable,[15] that the small producers are at the mercy of those who discard the materials, or what? If the small producers in a certain branch cannot expand beyond the scrap availability of some particular large firms then indeed there would be an important binding constraint. Probably this applies even more if the small producers depend on illegally obtained materials, a point made by King (1974). Thus access to raw materials is rightly stressed as a critical factor,[16] but the extent and the way in which this mitigates against the small producers still needs to be explicitly and carefully differentiated.

This latter point needs to be made in relation to Gerry's work in general, considering the absolute nature of his conclusions. It is worth quoting them in detail because they centrally address the issues in debate:

> Areas available for the expansion of petty production are determined by the sectors already controlled by capitalist production; the extent to which indigenous petty producers are transformed into small capitalists is thereby very limited. The entrenchment of capitalism in the decisive production process also limits the avenues available for small capitalist development. Not only is capitalist hegemony exercised over the decisive industrial sectors, but control over the institutional means of capital accumulation (i.e. credit facilities, contracts, licenses etc.) resides in the hands of the domestic bourgeoisie, whose interests are intimately linked to those of the metropolitan capitalist class. (1978, p.1154)
> Petty producers bear the cost and responsibility of absorbing much labour for which capitalism has no use, and are cruelly exploited through the price system, through contracting, and through legislated discrimination. (p.1156)
> More and more enterprises are forced to underutilise the skills available to them, to use

increasing amounts of low quality inputs ....
Each generation of petty producers that
undergoes this insidious marginalisation loses a
portion of its accumulated skills. (p.1158)

Petty production is therefore trapped in an
involutionary impasse, able only to reproduce
its conditions of existence, often at the expense
of its own standard of living and labour
remuneration. (p.1154)

While fully agreeing with Gerry's underlying approach
which focussed on the relationships between petty and
capitalist producers, one has to be cautious with his
conclusions because the impression is given that they can
be drawn from the information collected. A detailed
examination of his various papers reveals that the evidence
is far from conclusive. Hence the above quoted statements
should be regarded as hypotheses rather than research
results.

Access to Credit

Those contributions which (rightly or wrongly) express a
more optimistic view usually include suggestions for easier
access to credit (e.g. UNIDO, 1970; Fuenzalida, 1976). The
obstacles to the financing of small-scale producers are well
known. Commercial credit institutions are reluctant to
grant loans beause they consider the security offered by
the small producers as inadequate. Hence the latter resort
to other money lenders and pay higher interest rates than
large firms. A study on small-scale industry in Mexico, for
instance, reveals that these interest rates are between two
and eight times those charged by the official banks and
lending institutions (PREALC, 1979). Such differences can
hardly be explained by higher administrative costs which
banks incur in lending to small firms.

A study on the informal sector of Freetown, Sierra
Leone, brings out the problems in dealing with official
credit institutions as perceived by the small producers:
'Most entrepreneurs at this level of business activity see
banks and other financial institutions as impersonal and

hostile structures' which 'exist for foreign business and powerful indigenous figures' (Fowler, 1978, p.25). The majority of the respondents of this study emphasised the lack of loan and credit facilities as their most difficult obstacle.

The main question here is whether the higher interest rates paid by the small producers and their difficulties in gaining access to credit merely reflect an underlying reality of unstable and risky conditions of production (and hence repayment defaults) or whether they are due to distortions in the views and practices of those in charge of the credit institutions. Hans Singer, chief of the ILO Kenya Mission, strongly advocates the latter. He sees discrimination against the small producers not only in questions of credit but suggests that in general 'the dice are loaded against the informal sector due to government policies' (in conversation with the author).

Government Discrimination

The ILO Kenya Report (1972) is very explicit on this point.[17]

> One important characteristic of the formal sector is its relationship to the Government. Economic activities formally and officially recognised and fostered by the Government enjoy considerable advantages. First they obtain the direct benefits of access to credit, foreign exchange concessions, work permits for foreign technicians, and a formidable list of benefits that reduce costs of capital in relation to that of labour. Indirectly, establishments in the formal sector benefit immeasurably from the restriction of competition through tariffs, quotas, trade licensing and product and construction standards drawn from the rich countries or based on their criteria. Partly because of its privileged access to resources, the formal sector is characterised by large enterprise, sophisticated technology, high wage

34

rates, high average profits and foreign ownership.

The informal sector, on the other hand, is often ignored and in some respects helped and in some harassed by the authorities. Enterprises and individuals within it operate largely outside the system of government benefits and regulation, and thus have no access to the formal credit institutions and the main sources of transfer of technology. Many of the economic agents in this sector operate illegally, though often pursuing similar economic activities to those in the formal sector – marketing foodstuffs and other consumer goods, carrying out the repair and maintenance of machinery and consumer durables and running transport, for example. Illegality here is generally due not to the nature of the economic activity but to an official limitation of access to legitimate activity. (p.504)

These passages of the report give crucial significance to the relations which the various types of producers have to the state. Thus they provide a step forward in that they locate the question of the growth potential of the small producer in a more political context. In order to explore this context, one is of course ultimately forced to raise deeper questions about the power structure in the country, in particular about the role of the state, the social classes it is based on, and the connections with international capital. The mission stopped short of doing this,[18] probably because the report was in the first instance addressed to the Kenyan Government. As mentioned earlier, the report was not just a research document but also a consultancy report which aimed to influence the attitudes of politicians, administrators and planners. This is also a likely explanation of why the analysis of the Mission is not easy to reconcile with the optimistic view underlying its recommendations.

This 'excuse' is not valid for many of the subsequent informal sector studies which repeat the recommendations of the Kenya Mission in one form or other, suggesting that the optimistic view is justified. However, a closer analysis of these studies shows that the data collected can in most cases neither confirm nor contradict this view for a combination of reasons:

- they are based on one-off cross-section surveys, and/or

- they investigate individuals rather than enterprises, and

- they do not subject the 'external' context in which the small producers operate to empirical investigation.

This methodological issue is of great importance in evaluating a good part of the recent literature and it will be dealt with later in a separate section (3.4).

1.2 Earnings in Small Enterprises

Our interest in the growth constraints of small-scale producers is ultimately derived from our interest in the earning opportunities they provide. Presumably the conditions of operation of the enterprise largely determine how much the owner can earn, how regular these earnings are, how hard he has to work (how many hours) in order to achieve this income and to what extent he has to rely on family labour; to a lesser extent they also determine the wage he can afford to pay wage workers, if he has any.

While there is now a considerable number of studies which provide information on employment and income of small producers, in many cases it is very difficult to relate these findings to the conditions of operation of their enterprises. This difficulty is connected with the methodological problems mentioned above. Keeping this proviso in mind, what does the available literature say? As in the previous section, we will concentrate on manufacturing, whenever the findings are broken down by type of activity.

The ILO Kenya Report emphasised the 'marked

contrasts between the relative security and (high) income levels of those with wage-earning jobs in the bigger firms and those self-employed in the informal sector' (ILO, 1972, p.7). A conclusion of the PREALC surveys is that the average income of 'informal sector workers ... is significantly lower than that of persons employed in the formal sector' (Souza and Tokman, 1976, p.361). In other studies low income was even made a defining characteristic, by delimiting the informal sector in terms of workers who earn less than a legal minimum wage (e.g. México, 1975; PREALC, 1978a, Part III, Chapter 4; Schaefer, 1976).[19]

Webb (1974) found that in Peru average earnings in the 'modern sector' were higher than in the 'urban traditional sector' (= sector comprising enterprises of less than five workers); however, he also drew attention to the high variance of income in the 'urban traditional sector'. Proprietors who had between one and four workers earned considerably more than factory workers, and self-employed men working on their own enjoyed a slightly higher income than male factory workers.

In a study on the urban self-employed in Tanzania, Bienefeld (1974) also emphasised that making generalisations about their income is a hazardous undertaking. He found wide variations between the various activities (crafts and manufacture, construction, shopkeeping, streetselling and others). On those engaged in crafts and manufacture, he concluded that their incomes are mostly on a par or even higher than incomes derived from wage employment; 62 per cent (of those repsondents who stated their income) earned more than the legal minimum wage, which was relatively high at the time (1971) and could be regarded as a 'basis of an economically viable permanent existence' (p.47). Twenty-four per cent of these respondents earned even more than two minimum wages (table 19).[20]

Fowler (1978) calculated that in Sierra Leone the petty manufacturers fare better, on the whole, than workers employed in larger enterprises. Further evidence is provided in a study on the informal sector in Mauritania's capital, Nouakchott (Nihan and Jourdain, 1978); 'after deducting all running costs, 92.6 per cent of entrepreneurs in the manufacturing sector are still left with a profit equal to or greater than the weekly wage of a skilled workman in the modern sector' (p.714). A similar study carried out in Lomé, Togo, concludes that 'taking into account their levels of skills, 72.9 per cent of the entrepreneurs (in the informal sector) probably make a better living than they would if they worked in the modern formal sector...' (Nihan, Demol and Jondoh, 1979, p.663). These findings gain further support in a number of studies on South Asian Cities quoted by McGee (1979).

Finally it is most interesting to have data on Nairobi which question the view of the 1972 Kenya Mission. House (1978) found that the average income of heads of informal enterprises in manufacturing was over three times the legal minimum wage (the findings for trade and services are similar). This is all the more noteworthy since 'enterprises were classified as belonging to the informal sector for the purposes of the survey if they operated out of a temporary structure or from no structure at all' (p.10). King (1974) calculated that a self-employed machine maker (without assistants) could earn in Nairobi twice the legal minimum wage.

Reliable information on income is generally the most difficult to come by. The percentage of non responses in surveys tends to be high on this question and there is always the likelihood that those who provide the information understate it. An equally serious problem is that the income declared by the head of the small enterprise can represent not only the remuneration of his own labour but also that of (unpaid) family labour; then there is the question of how much of his income represents return on the capital invested. Hence such information must be interpreted as merely providing some approximate orders of magnitude as a basis for discussion.

The significance of including or excluding family labour in calculations on earnings is revealed in statistics on small industries in West Bengal quoted by Bose (1978). They show that on average the income of the 'working proprietor' is 1.5 times the wage of a hired worker in that type of industry, but if a wage were imputed for the family labour used in his enterprise, his income would become negative. The same calculation, made for Calcutta city, shows that the average income of the 'working proprietor' is four times the wage of a hired worker (in small industry) while if a wage is imputed for the family labour used, the income is only 2.4 times that wage[21] (tables 9 and 10 in Bose, 1978).

An assessment of the wages paid to workers employed in small-scale enterprises also carries many difficulties.[22] The wage relationship tends to be overlaid with social ties and part of the wage is often paid in kind (especially in the form of board and lodging).

Studies on West Africa generally show the extensive use of apprentices at very low levels of remuneration. Steel (1977) found that in Accra, Ghana, 35 per cent of all workers were apprentices in small-scale manufacturing and repairs. Aryee (1977) found that in Kumasi, Ghana, apprentices accounted for 86 per cent of employees in small-scale manufacturing. Both conclude that the main reason for the engagement of apprentice labour is that it is cheap. According to Nihan and Jourdain (1978), 40 per cent of the workers in small-scale manufacturing in Nouakchott were apprentices. In Lomé the figure was 88 per cent and apprentices were found to earn on average 18 per cent of the minimum wage. The authors emphasised not so much the cheapness of this labour, but apprenticeship as a 'traditional and inexpensive training process which performs an important function as a preparation for self-employment and at the same time acts as a springboard to employment in the modern formal sector' (Nihan, Demol and Jondoh, 1979, p.633). Kennedy (1979), however, in a study on Accra points to the practice of unduly prolonging the apprenticeship period as a way of keeping 'extremely low paid workers' (p.24). Gerry (1979) stresses that the use of low-paid labour in the form of apprentices under paternalist and personalised relations of production is essential for the survival of the small-scale enterprises. As for other workers in these West African enterprises, information is more scarce. Fowler (1978) found that in Sierra Leone they receive wages well below the legal minimum wage. Nihan and co-researchers concluded that in the capitals of Mauritania and Togo most workers in small enterprises (who are not apprentices) earn more than the minimum wage (Nihan et al., 1978, 1979).

In most other studies only average wages for all workers are given. In the manufacturing industry of Colombia, wages in small enterprises were, according to 1958 data, significantly lower than those in larger enterprises (Nelson, Schultz and Slighton, 1971). In Mexican industry increasing disparities were found between wages in small-scale units and wages in larger firms over the period 1965-75 (PREALC, 1978b).[23]

In general, small-scale producers have the reputation of paying lower wages (Dhar and Lydall, 1961; ECLA, 1969). In fact when these small enterprises are subcontracted by larger firms one would expect this, and indeed it is a well documented fact (Staley and Morse, 1965). However, when these producers are not part of the production network of a large enterprise and work on their own account, one can assume that their internal division of labour is only very limited, that they therefore need workers with a wide range of skills and hence might have to pay wages which are at least comparable to those in larger firms.[24] But this point is rarely explored in the literature either at a theoretical or at an empirical level.

A basic problem in all these comparisons is that disaggregation is necessary not only for the small-scale sector but also for the large-scale sector. Averages for the workforce of large firms tend to hide wide differences in remuneration and other conditions of work. It is these differences which gave rise to the debate on the segmentation of labour markets, which is very extensive for the case of developed countries, in particular the United States,[25] but has also received increasing attention in relation to less developed countries. For example, in a study of the Bombay textile industry, Mazumdar (1973) found that alongside a stable core of workers with a relatively high wage, the industry employed a sizeable proportion of workers on casual day-to-day contracts and low wages. On the basis of this experience and other findings Mazumdar (1975) suggests a two-tier urban labour market which does not correspond to the small/large-scale dichotomy; the reason lies in the division within the

40

workforce of the <u>large</u> firms, one part of which is protected by trade unions and government legislation and which is relatively stable and well paid, while the other part is not.[26] This is not the place to review the literature on differences in employment conditions within the large-scale sector. The points which are pertinent for our discussion are that, first, comparisons between remuneration in large and in small enterprises are much more problematic than appears from the quoted studies, and second, the workforce in large firms is not as privileged as often alleged, at least not in its entirety.

For the sake of convenience many researchers take, as we have seen above, the legal minimum wage as the yardstick for earnings in the small-scale sector. This can be a meaningful way of proceeding in a specific country at a specific time, but it is rather problematic if one wants to assess changes over time or differences between countries. While the minimum wage in say Kenya or Tanzania in 1971 was relatively high and enabled a worker and his family to make a decent living, the minimum wage in Brazil in the same year was barely sufficient for the survival of a worker, let alone his family. In contrast, the Brazilian minimum wage in the mid-fifties came close to covering the costs of reproduction of the worker and his dependents.

Finally, in order to assess correctly the earnings in the small-scale sector and compare them with those in larger firms one would need additional information on the length of the working day, number of days worked per week, observance of public holidays and also on the regularity of work in small enterprises. Data on these aspects are even more patchy than on earnings, and in the few cases where they are available there is rarely a comparison with the conditions in the larger enterprises, making interpretation very difficult.[27]

By way of concluding this section it must be stated that no clear-cut picture of the earnings in the small-scale sector arises. However, one should emphasise that the image of the small-scale sector as that of the poor, and the large-scale sector as that of the privileged, is questionable. To some extent this characterisation has emerged because of the way the sectors were defined or because of lack of disaggregation.

Probably the most critical issue is one of separating the heads or owners of enterprises from the wage workers. While the owner might work the same number of hours as his wage worker (or even more), the difference in earnings is likely to be substantial. As we have seen, there is evidence from several studies that those who set up their own little business earn incomes higher than those of comparable wage workers in large enterprises. This would throw serious doubt on the view, so prominent in the informal sector discussion, that these small-scale activities are a stepping stone or gateway to wage employment.[28]

In fact there is further evidence that the small producers are <u>not</u> frustrated job seekers who strive towards, but cannot get, employment in larger enterprises. Nihan et al. (1978, 1979) suggest that a good number of the small producers used to be wage workers in the larger firms. This is confirmed by House (1978) who also found that most of the small-scale manufacturers seek no change in occupation. Sit, Wong and Kiang (1979) report on Hong Kong that 'there existed a strong connection between their first job and their subsequent entrepreneurial career in that very often both were in the same field of manufacture. It seems as though they chose a job with a view on that industry's growth potential and the prospect of acquiring sufficient know-how to set up on their own in the future' (p.294). This is in line with Peattie's (1978) impressions of shoe manufacturing in Colombia where employers complained that as soon as workers became well-trained, they left to start workshops of their own; ownership of a small workshop appeared as a desirable position - relative to the other available options.

> Small enterprises constitute a way in which those at the bottom of the system can command and aggregate resources. They provide for those without educational credentials not the surety of upward mobility, but more of a possibility for mobility than they would find as unskilled or semi-skilled labour in a big firm. Even without the mobility, they

provide a setting in which those with minimal status resources can have the prideful sense of being "independent".

To the academic observer, his career built around tenure security, these advantages may seem illusory, in any case an inadequate recompense for long hours, hard work, low earnings. From my discussions with petty entrepreneurs and small manufacturers in Bogotá, I am convinced that these satisfactions and possibilities are real, and not to be minimised. (pp.32-3)[29]

It would seem that further empirical investigation of this issue is highly important for our understanding of the emergence of small enterprises and the vicissitudes in the process of proletarianisation.

Finally, this issue has considerable bearing on our initial discussion on growth prospects. Expansion can hardly be expected from small enterprises whose owner would pack up at the first opportunity of wage employment in a larger firm. In this sense, findings which indicate that the small-scale sector is not a waiting room occupied by those who have not yet been able to find such wage employment are important.[30] Second, findings that small enterprises are set up by skilled workers would indicate that entry into these small-scale activities is not as unrestricted as often alleged.[31]

Notes

1 Adopting a term coined previously by Hart (1971).
2 For a discussion of small-scale rural non-farm activities see Chuta and Liedholm (1979) and UNIDO (1979, Chapter XII). Recent studies which concentrate on urban small-scale trade and services include Bromley (1978b), Cavalcanti (1978), McGee and Yeung (1977), Marga Institute (1978), Möller (1976), Moser (1977), PREALC (1978c).
3 Watanabe (1970) attributes the rapid industrialisation of Japan to the widespread entrepreneurship which could

unfold in the large number of small-scale enterprises. He suggests that the problem of industrialisation in developing countries is in the first instance one of creating conditions 'which activate the existing entrepreneurial resources that are lying dormant' (p.532). The real issue, of course, is to agree on the conditions which are required if this entrepreneurship is to unfold.

4   In contrast to Kilby, Stepanek believes the 'problem' can be rectified by training courses and most of his book, Managers for Small Industry (1960), is devoted to suggestions for management training programmes.

5   House (1978) refers to an unpublished study by P. Henning on the 'analysis of household budgets and expenditures on informal sector products in an urban uncontrolled housing settlement' which may have covered parts of the question but was not available.

6   Data on family expenditure alone cannot, of course, clarify the issue in debate because a high percentage of expenditure on industrialised goods could be due to the cheapness of wage goods brought from small producers.

7   Alves de Souza and Carvalho (1977) in a paper which refers to the same city as that studied by Prandi, namely Salvador, put forward a more differentiated view, which is further supported by a study on the informal sector in Recife by Cavalcanti (1978).

8   At least to the extent that they are under real pressure to provide these services.

9   Some parts of Kowarick's work on urban marginality (1975) suggest this position, but he does not distinguish between domestic subsistence production and the production of marketed wage goods which would seem to be an important step towards clarifying the theoretical and empirical problems involved. For a discussion of further questions raised in this thorny debate see Bennholdt-Thomsen (1979) and Souza (1979).

10   We shall return to this theme in section 3.4.

11   This is however not supported by the results of a cross-section study by Ozorio de Almeida (1976) based on Brazilian industrial census data. She suggests that 'industrial subcontracting of low-skill service workers occurs mostly in the early stages of industrialisation, when

firms are still relatively small and when labour-intensive functions are not yet well organised. As industrialisation takes hold, and as average scale of operation increases, the organisational difficulties of subcontracting begin to mount and intermittent workers come to be increasingly replaced by permanent industrial employees' (p.218).

12   For a review of the very extensive Japanese literature on the subject see Shinohara (1968).

13   Further case studies in other countries have been carried out in connection with Watanabe's research project, but the results were not available at the time of writing.

14   We are not considering here the repair services investigated by Gerry.

15   For instance, Birkbeck (1979) shows that garbage pickers in Cali collected such an amount of waste paper that it formed a steady supply used by Colombia's main paper producing company.

16   Also emphasised by Steel (1977).

17   This discriminatory dimension was particularly emphasised in John Weeks' submission to the ILO Kenya Report. See also Weeks (1973, 1975).

18   This is Leys' (1975) main critique of the report.

19   Such definition aggravated the conceptual confusion in the informal sector debate.

20   In the context of this discussion there are frequent references in the literature to a study by Merrick (1976), 'Employment and Earnings in the Informal Sector in Brazil: The Case of Belo Horizonte'. These references are generally misguided because of Merrick's definition of the informal sector, which is in terms of persons 'who did not contribute to social security institutes' (p.340). Our own experience suggests that in the Brazilian context this is likely to lead to the exclusion of a considerable number of small-scale producers and at the same time to the inclusion of workers of larger enterprises in the 'informal sector' so defined.

21   Of course one must be clear about the purpose of such deduction. If made for welfare comparisons, it has little meaning especially if there is no alternative employment for the family members. The matter is different if one is interested in value comparisons.   Both questions will be

taken up again in Part 3.

22 The extent of wage employment as opposed to self-employment depends, of course, largely on one's delimitation of the small-scale or informal sector.

23 This study does not include enterprises of less than six workers. However, according to estimates by Garcia (1978), the same tendency applies to those enterprises with up to five workers.

24 Certainly the wage differentials, to the extent that they do exist, can hardly be explained by lower skill requirements in small-scale manufacturing.

25 For a review see Cain (1976).

26 Mazumdar used the labels 'formal-informal' for this dichotomy which is unfortunate in that it further contributed to the confusion surrounding this concept; this does not however invalidate his emphasis on the differentiation of the labour force within the large-scale sector. A similar distinction of the labour market of less developed countries was suggested by Dore (1974) which arose from his research on Japan (1973) and was empirically investigated in Senegal (Mackintosh, 1975) and Mexico (Sanchez Padron, 1975).

27 For a discussion on duration of work see Myrdal (1968, Chapter 23).

28 As implied in e.g. ILO (1972), Sethuraman (1976), Souza and Tokman (1976).

29 A similar view in relation to tertiary activities is put forward by Peattie (1975).

30 This is further supported by Bienefeld (1974), Webb (1974), Martine and Peliano (1978), and others who show that the small-scale activities are not carried out typically by recent migrants.

31 Especially in PREALC (1978a).

PART 2

CASE STUDIES FROM BRAZIL

The objective of this part of the work is to present three case studies in which the issues raised in the first part can be examined.

2.1 The Approach

The research approach adopted for these case studies rests on three premises:

(1) while our ultimate concern is the employment and income of people, the unit of analysis should be the enterprise whose condition of operation determines the availability and terms of work;

(2) at our present state of knowledge we cannot sensibly investigate these conditions of operation for the small-scale sector as a whole, and the most fruitful way of proceeding is through research by branch of activity;

(3) these branch studies have to include both small and large enterprises, as the relationships between them are likely to be crucial determinants of the conditions of production and employment in the small enterprises.

There are advantages to setting up research in this way, but also limitations. Rather than discussing these in the abstract we prefer to present first our material and later (in section 3.4) discuss the merits and shortcomings of the case study approach which focusses on the branch. Here we merely wish to emphasise the need to 'get a grip' on the workings of the entire branch in which the small enterprises operate in order to correctly evaluate their conditions of production and employment. By 'small enterprises' we mean those with up to ten workers. This dividing line was chosen because it is the most widely used cut-off point in the recent debate.

The three case studies are drawn from the manufacturing industry in Brazil and will be presented in the following order:

(1)   the knitting and clothing industry of Petrópolis in the state of Rio de Janeiro,

(2)   the hammock industry of Fortaleza in the state of Ceará,

(3)   the weaving industry of Americana in the state of São Paulo.

All three industries belong to the textile sector in the wider sense. This sector was chosen, first, because the textile and clòthing industry together account for the highest share in manufacturing employment in Brazil. Second, it was known to include branches in which small-scale enterprises are important. Third, it is a very heterogeneous sector and three branches were chosen which had attained different levels of technological development: in the production of hammocks, technology has virtually stagnated and most operations are still done manually; the clothing industry has seen a considerable increase in the efficiency of machines, but production is still largely organised on the basis of one operator per machine; the weaving industry has experienced a rapid change from labour-intensive to capital-intensive methods, with a rapid rise in the number of machines which can be operated by one person and the continual improvement of these machines.

Some explanation is necessary about the selection of firms and the collection of information. The larger enterprises were selected at random from enterprise registers. In the case of the small ones, however, we often had to rely on informal contacts since most producers were clandestine and did not appear on any register.[1] Hence the sampling universe could not be known. Consequently it is difficult to estimate how representative the sample was, but this problem was alleviated in a number of ways. First, in the interviews, discussion was not restricted solely to the enterprise in question, but an attempt was made to establish the extent to which the findings on that enterprise were perceived as typical or generalisable by the respondents. Second, the large producers were asked about the workings of the small ones and vice versa. Third, great importance was attached to the information of those who were not producers themselves, but occupied key positions in the industry, namely the suppliers of machinery and raw material. They tended to have both firm-specific knowledge and, what was more important, a <u>general</u> view of the structure and workings of the branch. In drawing on these various sources it was possible to limit the danger of drawing conclusions from a possibly unrepresentative sample.[2]

Within the selected enterprises interviews were conducted with their owners or managers. They took between two and four hours and were held in free conversational form, but followed a set of predetermined questions;[3] some interviews were recorded with the permission of the respondent. Within each place of work, direct observation was an additional means of interpreting or querying some of the information given. This took the form of a visit to the factory or workshop which lasted between thirty minutes and two hours, depending on its size, the knowledge already gained in previous visits to other firms, and the degree of cooperation obtained.

While each of the three case studies is in some sense independent, there is a common pattern in their presentation: following the general statistics and estimates of the relative importance of the branch in general and of small-scale production within it, an initial idea is provided of the structure of the industry in question. This is followed by detailed examination of the factors concerning the growth, survival or destruction of the small producers, and by an assessment of the employment and income conditions which arise from this. This part of the work is limited to a presentation of the results of the fieldwork. Some of the wider implications of the results will be discussed in Part 3.

2.2 The Brazilian Setting

Before plunging into the case studies, they should be
situated in their 'macro context'; to this end we will briefly
review the recent record of the Brazilian economy in terms
of economic growth, employment and income distribution
and the general development of production and
employment in the industries investigated.

Economic Growth, Employment and Income in Brazil

The performance of the Brazilian economy after the
military take-over in 1964 is a prime example of the
possibility of dependent but dynamic capitalist
development (Cardoso, 1974, 1975, Chapter II). Among the
main features of this development have been fast rates of
economic growth and a worsening distribution of income,
achieved under an 'alliance of multinational, state and
local capital' (Evans, 1979). There has been an extensive
debate on how to interpret this rapid growth (e.g. Bacha,
1977; Malan and Bonelli, 1977), how uneven the income
distribution actually is (e.g. Suplicy et al., 1978;
Pfeffermann and Webb, 1979) and where the interests of
foreign and national capital clash or coincide (e.g.
Bandeira, 1975; Evans, 1979).[4] This is not the place to
review or enter these debates; for the purpose of this work
it suffices to give some orders of magnitude of recent
developments.

The Brazilian economy has had an impressive growth
record in particular during the decade 1965-75 when its
average yearly growth rate (GDP) surpassed the 10 per
cent mark (see Table 1). During 1960-70 this rate was 2.2
times the yearly increase in population and over the period
1965-75 it was 3.7 times as high. From 1964 (when the new
'Brazilian model' was set up) to 1977 the per capita income
increased by 5.2 per cent yearly (IPEA, 1978).

The fast rate of growth of the economy favoured the
creation of jobs, but during the sixties the increase in
employment remained below the increase in the
economically active population (see Table 2). However,
over the period 1972-76, the latter was slightly overtaken

TABLE 1   Growth of the economy and population, 1960–75

Year	GDP (in Cr$ millions and 1975 prices)	Population (millions)
1960	274.8	67.8
1965	373.7	81.0
1970	555.1	93.4
1975	1009.4	107.1
1960–70	6.6% p.a.	2.9% p.a.
1965–75	10.4% p.a.	2.8% p.a.

Source: Instituto Brasileiro de Geografia e Estatística (IBGE) and Fundação Getúlio Vargas (FGV); figures quoted from Centro Nacional de Recursos Humanos (CNRH, 1978).

by employment growth, suggesting that the fast economic growth did not fail to leave its mark on employment generation. This is further supported by the decrease in 'visible underemployment' which shows that the percentage of persons working less than forty hours weekly fell from 1970 to 1976. Caution is however necessary in interpreting such macro-economic indicators, especially in relation to the rate of 'invisible underemployment' which also decreased (Table 2). The latter is a poverty indicator, rather than an indicator of underemployment, being defined in terms of number of people who earn up to one minimum wage. This minimum wage actually fell from 1960 to 1976 by about half, the exact amount varies with the deflator used.[5] According to the trade union research institute (DIEESE, 1977) the minimum wage continued to fall over the period 1972–76, whereas the Government claimed a slight improvement (IPEA, 1978).

While the exact relationship between the official minimum wage and actually paid wages varies between

TABLE 2 Changes in economically active population, employment and underemployment, 1960–76

(percentages)

	1960–70	1972–76
Economically active population - average yearly increase	2.7	3.0
Employment - average yearly increase	2.5	3.2

	1970	1972	1976
Underemployment - rate of 'visible underemployment'	17.7	17.7	12.3
- rate of 'invisible underemployment'	60.5	52.4	37.1

Source: IBGE, Censo Demográfico for 1960 and 1970, Pesquisa Nacional de Amostra de Domícilios (PNAD) for 1972 and 1976; figures quoted from CNRH (1978, 1979).

regions, industries and types of workers,[6] an indication should be given of what the minimum wage means in subsistence terms. (This is important in the context of our work because in accordance with Brazilian practice we will frequently refer to this wage and express the remuneration of labour in multiples of the minimum wage.) If one considers the basic needs of food, housing, clothing, hygiene and transport of a working class family in São Paulo in 1976/77, the minimum wage is at best sufficient to cover the expenses of the worker himself, but totally inadequate to guarantee the subsistence of his family (Calsing, 1978). The inadequacy of the minimum wage and increasing difficulties in access to housing and sanitation find their most sombre expression in increases in the infant mortality rate in the late sixties and early seventies

(Kowarick, 1977; Bacha, 1977).

There is little doubt that the government policy of repressing labour unions or any other form of opposition contributed to this development. Under this policy a worsening of the distribution of income is hardly surprising. As we can see from Table 3, the share of the richest 5 per cent in total income, which had already increased from 27.7 per cent in 1960 to 34.9 in 1970, increased even further to 39 in 1976. In contrast, 80 per cent of the population lost out, most notably the poorest 50 per cent had their shares reduced from 17.7 in 1960 to 11.8 per cent in 1976. As a result the Gini-coefficient increased from 0.50 in 1960 to 0.60 in 1976.

TABLE 3 Distribution of income, 1960, 1970, 1976

Economically active population	Income shares (percentages)		
	1960	1970	1976
Poorest 50 per cent	17.7	14.9	11.8
Following 30 per cent	27.9	22.8	21.2
Following 15 per cent	26.7	27.4	28.0
Richest 5 per cent	27.7	34.9	39.0
Total 100 per cent	100.0	100.0	100.0
Gini-coefficient	0.50	0.56	0.60

Source: IBGE, Censo Demográfico for 1960 and 1970 and PNAD for 1976; figures quoted from Serra (1978).

The sharpening of inequality in the country can also be observed in Table 4 which shows that the increase in average income of the poor was below that of the rich. While the poorest 50 per cent managed to increase their average income in the period 1970 to 1976 more quickly than in the sixties, the rate of increase was only half that of the richest 5 per cent. Nevertheless, the data show that the poor also improved their income. Its absolute level, however, remained very low; in 1976 the average income of the poorest 50 per cent was still only at minimum wage level (CNRH, 1978).

TABLE 4 Growth rates of average real incomes, 1960–76

(percentages)

Economically active population	1960–70	1970–76
Poorest 50 per cent	15.5	65.6
Following 30 per cent	12.5	93.8
Following 15 per cent	40.5	113.7
Richest 5 per cent	75.4	133.7

Source: see Table 3.

The political conditions enforced by the military government made Brazil one of the favourites of international capital. Today foreign capital dominates the following branches of manufacturing industry: chemicals and pharmaceuticals, electrical and communication equipment, transportation equipment (especially the car industry), machinery, rubber products and tobacco. In some of these, such as pharmaceuticals or electrical equipment, foreign capital reached its position through denational-isation[7] (Evans, 1979; Newfarmer, 1979);[8] in others such as the car industry, there was no displacement of local producers insofar as entirely new product lines were introduced. Local capital maintained its stronghold, most notably in metallurgy, wood products and furniture, food and beverages, printing and publishing, paper products and also in the industries studied in this work; 82 per cent of the capital invested in textiles is under national control and in clothing it reaches 96 per cent (Visão, 1977).

Production and Employment in Textile and Clothing

The position of local capital in textiles is linked to its long history.[9] The first Brazilian mills were founded in the middle of the last century and by the beginning of this century local capital had begun to supplant imports. From then on until the middle of the twenties was the 'golden age' of the industry. During this period many of today's leading Brazilian firms were established and local production catered for over 95 per cent of internal consumption. After a period of decline in the second half of the twenties, production rose gradually during the thirties. There was a boom during the Second World War when Brazil supplied all its domestic needs and exported to various countries. After the war production fell, but picked up again in the fifties and has since oscillated around a trend of only modest growth, well below average industrial expansion in the country. This meant that the share of textiles in industrial production fell from 19 per cent in 1950 to 9 in 1970, and in industrial employment from 26 per cent in 1950 to 13 in 1970. Growth continued to be slow over the years of most rapid expansion of the Brazilian economy; thus from 1970 to 1974 production increased by only 16 per cent compared with 61 per cent in manufacturing industry overall; employment increased by only 5 per cent compared with 30 per cent in industry in general. Even a rise in the exports of yarn and cloth by almost 800 per cent over these four years could not substantially alter the limits which internal income distribution put on the expansion of the industry.

As a result of this slow growth, the textile industry is ranked in the Brazilian industrialisation literature amongst the 'traditional' industries which are contrasted to the 'dynamic' industries (e.g. Viceconti, 1977). The latter are associated with high growth rates of output, but also with advanced capital-intensive technology. While the conservatism of local mill owners and the obsolescence of machinery, especially up to the sixties, confirmed the reputation of textiles as a traditional industry, today this characterisation conceals more than it reveals: stagnation in some subbranches coexists with record growth rates in others; firms which employ the most advanced technology by world standards coexist with others whose equipment looks obsolete. The reasons are linked to the peculiarity of the textile market which is very compartmentalised in terms of products, marketing channels and regions. In this sense, a recent research report correctly criticises those studies which centre on the idea of textiles as a traditional industry and points to their 'inability to understand the complex character of the unevenness in the textile industry' (Tavares and Pereira, 1976, p.55). Therefore, as the interest of our research does not lie in the textile industry as such, no attempt will be made to provide a more extensive general survey on the industry. Instead we will try within each case study to give the specific context which is necessary to understand the branch concerned and the small-scale producers who operate within it.

However, given the concern with employment in this work and in particular with the role of small enterprises in providing employment, we will look in some detail at the employment statistics, differentiating between the three branches to be analysed in the case studies: weaving, clothing and hammocks. Unfortunately the data base is highly deficient, but again the main objective is to provide some orders of magnitude. The total in Table 5 shows the slow growth of employment mentioned before, but nevertheless textiles (which includes weaving and hammocks) and clothing together account for the highest share (16 per cent) in industrial employment.[10]

TABLE 5   Workers in the textile and clothing industry, 1950-70

Industry	1950	1960	1970
Textiles	368,960	328,297	342,839
Clothing	19,344	33,244	77,837
Total	388,304	361,541	420,676

Source: IBGE, Censo Industrial.

56

Let us first look at the clothing industry. A problem with the employment statistics for this industry is that a proportion of the clothing workers are included in the statistics on the textile industry, namely those involved in knitted clothing. In Table 6 we have added these to the clothing workers already listed in Table 5.

TABLE 6 Workers in the clothing industry (including knitwear), 1950-70

Year	1950	1960	1970
Workers	26,557	45,174	112,626

Source: IBGE, Censo Industrial.

However, even these adjusted figures still underestimate the real number of workers involved in clothing production. One can reach this conclusion by contrasting the figures in Table 6 with those on occupation contained in the Demographic Census, according to which the numbers of 'tailors and seamstresses' were as shown in Table 7.

TABLE 7 Tailors and seamstresses, 1950-70

Year	1950	1960	1970
Workers	257,804	388,814	405,328

Source: IBGE, Censo Demográfico.

There are several problems in using these figures as indicators for employment in the clothing industry. For example, the industry does not only employ workers who work on sewing machines; from this point of view the figures are too low. On the other hand, some of the tailors and seamstresses are engaged in the repair of clothes rather than production of new clothes. Also not all work full time in this occupation, but according to the Census, 76 per cent work 40 hours per week or more. These and other problems have been discussed elsewhere (Schmitz, 1978) in a detailed examination of the relevant data of the Industrial, Services and Demographic Censuses. The conclusion reached was that the total number of people engaged in clothing production in 1970 was probably around three times the number given in the Industrial Census. It should be emphasised that this conclusion was based on some rather crude estimates, but in all likelihood they constitute a lesser evil than taking the Industrial Census figures at face value.[11]

The question arises as to why the Industrial Census is so inadequate. First, it does not cover outworkers which is a serious omission in the case of the clothing industry.[12] Second, it leaves out many small-scale enterprises, largely because they are not registered. For instance, for the entire state of Rio de Janeiro a mere thirty knitting and twenty-five clothing firms of less than five workers were listed (in 1970), whereas in Petrópolis alone (town in that state) hundreds of such small enterprises existed according to our informants. Thus the Industrial Census gives at best an indication of the size of the <u>internal</u> workforce of the medium and large enterprises. Interpreting Table 6 in this light, we can conclude that this workforce increased substantially over the period 1950 to 1970. How total employment in the small-scale sector developed is hard to say. Casual observation would suggest that there are two conflicting tendencies. On the one hand, production of garments made <u>to measure</u> for private customers seems to be declining. On the other hand, there are signs of a considerable increase of small workshops which produce clothes <u>in series</u>, be it for large clothing firms, for shops or itinerant salesmen.[13]

The data problem in the hammock industry is similar to that in the clothing industry. Although a relatively small textile branch, its real importance for employment is far greater than suggested by official figures.[14] We made an estimate of the total number of workers for one of the main centres of production which is included as an annex to the case study. This estimate was compared with the most recent official figures available, with the result that these proved to cover at best one-sixth of the real workforce. Even though our estimate again involves a number of daring assumptions, it is undoubtedly closer to reality than the official figures.

Let us now turn to the employment statistics on the weaving industry, which has to be considered in conjunction with the spinning industry since many mills have integrated both operations and statistically it is very difficult to separate them. Spinning and weaving is the most important textile branch, even though employment has decreased as shown in Table 8.

TABLE 8   Workers in the spinning and weaving industry, 1950-70

Year	1950	1960	1970
Workers	242,206	213,060	193,514

Source: IBGE, Censo Industrial.

The absolute decline in employment is due to technical change which affected the industry in particular from the sixties onwards. For one region an attempt was made to study this change in employment in some detail, though based on secondary sources. We chose to do this for the North East, where the industry underwent the most dramatic change. The spinning and weaving industry in this region was, at the end of the fifties, the country's most backward in technological terms (SUDENE, 1961; ECLA, 1963); today it is amongst its most advanced. The decisive decade was that of the sixties when the government, through the regional planning authority SUDENE, initiated a massive re-equipment programme. According to the

Industrial Census, employment in the spinning and weaving industry was cut by almost half (46 per cent) over this decade. SUDENE (1971) itself carried out a survey to assess the impact of its policy and reached the conclusion that the net employment effect was a decline of only 4 per cent, that is, employment hardly changed.

Provoked by this substantial difference, we examined both sources in detail (Schmitz, 1979a), and confirmed that both did in fact cover the same universe. However, no conclusion could be reached as to which result reflected what really happened, not even in discussions with those who had been responsible for the data collection on this industry. Also, both sources are quoted in the literature, giving rise to very different conclusions.[15] What is worse, the data examined and the inconsistencies refer to medium and large-scale enterprises for which one would not expect such discrepancies. It is impossible to say what happened in the small-scale sector on the basis of the available information. Significantly SUDENE itself did not even attempt to cover it in its surveys.

These examples are not meant to suggest that the official data are useless. They are to stress the dangers which are involved in basing a detailed survey on employment in the Brazilian textile and clothing industry on such data. The problems are particularly severe for small-scale firms, but they are by no means limited to this stratum of enterprises.[16] However, even accepting the statistics as they stand, they show that together these industries account for the highest share in industrial employment, as pointed out already.

In this Brazil is no exception. On the contrary, the average share of these industries in industrial employment of less developed countries is even higher, as can be seen from Table 9. Unfortunately the clothing industry is listed together with the shoe industry, but it is interesting to note that together textiles, clothing and shoes make up a third of industrial employment in developing countries, compared with 15 per cent in developed countries.

The general importance of small-scale enterprises in these industries is underlined in Table 10. In less developed countries, enterprises of up to nine workers account for a

| | Industrial employment | | | |
| | Developed economies | | Less developed economies | |
Branch of activity	Percentage weight 1970	Annual rate of growth 1962-74	Percentage weight 1970	Annual rate of growth 1962-73
Food, beverages and tobacco	10.2	0.4	19.0	3.3
Textiles	7.6	-1.3	22.3	3.0
Wearing apparel, leather and footwear	7.5	1.1	10.8	6.2
Wood products and furniture	5.9	1.3	8.1	5.2
Paper, printing and publishing	7.0	1.2	3.0	4.0
Chemical, petroleum, plastic products	8.6	2.0	5.7	5.6
Non-metallic mineral products	4.1	0.6	6.0	4.7
Basic metal industries	5.9	0.7	2.2	5.6
Metal products, machinery and equipment	34.8	1.8	11.4	6.2
Other industries	1.8	-	3.3	-
Light manufacturing	40.1	0.7	68.2	4.2
Heavy manufacturing	55.3	0.9	23.6	5.6
Manufacturing (total)	93.4	1.1	91.8	4.5
Mining and quarrying	3.7	-3.2	5.6	1.8
Electricity, gas and water	2.9	1.1	2.6	4.7
All industry	100.0	1.0	100.0	4.4

Source: United Nations, *Yearbook of Industrial Statistics*, 1974 edition, Vol. I, Part II, New York, 1976.

TABLE 10 Share of small-scale enterprises in industrial employment in sample of developed and less developed countries by industry groups[a]

(percentages)

Industry group	Industrial composition	Employment share		
		Weighted average share of small enterprises[b]		
		A	B	C
Developed countries sample				
Industry group I	30	5.1	13.5	39.1
Industry group II	14	2.9	9.0	28.7
Industry group III	56	1.3	4.2	15.4
Total	100	3.7	8.5	24.4
Less developed countries sample				
Industry group I	43	22.4	32.3	53.1
Industry group II	27	24.0	33.6	45.7
Industry group III	30	13.6	21.8	36.6
Total	100	19.0	31.4	52.0

Notes:

a   Industry group I: food, beverages, wood, furniture, printing and publishing, non-metallic mineral products and diverse. Industry group II: textiles, clothing and leather. Industry group III: paper, rubber, chemicals, petroleum, basic metals, fabricated metals, non-electrical machinery, electrical machinery and transport equipment.

b   A, B and C are three alternative definitions of small scale, namely enterprise in the scale range of 1-4, 1-9 and 1-49 workers respectively.

Source: national censuses; figures quoted from Banerji (1978).

third of employment in these industries. Obviously one does not want to read too much into such international cross-section data, but if the Brazilian experience reported above is anything to go by, the employment shares of small enterprises in this table are unlikely to be underestimates.

2.3 The Knitting and Clothing Industry of Petrópolis

Our first contacts with the real world were most illuminating. They revealed an increasing number of small enterprises, set up not by unsuccessful job seekers with no alternative, but by relatively skilled workers attempting to improve their economic and social situation. Some of the external obstacles emphasised in the literature turned out to be real; they made accumulation very difficult, but nevertheless some small producers seemed able to grow.

These features emerged quite clearly in the course of the interviews,[17] but it became equally clear that documenting this situation would not b easy. In the branch selected, knitted clothing, the small-scale sector was to a large extent clandestine, so virtually no secondary information of a qualitative or quantitative kind was available. In addition, changing fashions, seasons and a very diffuse distribution network were particularly marked in this branch: product differentiation was enormous as was the speed at which the cycle of ordering - buying raw material - producing - delivering took place. The basis of survival of the small producers seemed to lie in the very 'anarchy' of the prevailing production and marketing practices. In fact, our first respondent told us, 'if you ask me what I'll be doing next week, I can't tell you ... everything here is short-term and improvised.' This was reinforced by his scepticism about the possibilities of helping the small producers through any form of association: 'organising them all would only work if they were to produce suits and military uniforms.'

Originally the study on this branch was to serve as a kind of pilot study in order to learn the best ways of tracing small, often clandestine, producers; ways of obtaining their cooperation; possibilities of learning indirectly about them (e.g. through suppliers); and ways of improving our interview schedule . Nevertheless, it is believed that the relatively small case study which emerged throws some interesting light on several issues raised in the earlier debate, even though the information collected is largely of a qualitative nature. It should be repeated that in this and the following more extensive case studies only the findings are presented without explicit reference to the literature. The general implications of these findings will be discussed in Part 3.

The information for the first study was gathered from: three large firms with more than 100 workers; five medium firms of less than 100 but more than ten workers, most of them in the range of eleven to fifty workers; five small firms with up to ten (usually family) workers; the principal supplier of machinery and equipment to small producers; and a dealer in raw materials (yarn), serving mainly the small producers. Access to unregistered enterprises was greatly facilitated by the help received from the machinery supplier.[18]

The Growth of Knitted Clothing in Petrópolis

The research was carried out in Petrópolis, a medium-sized town in the state of Rio de Janeiro with a population of approximately 150,000. It is located in the mountains one-and-a-half hours' drive from the city of Rio on the coast. The town is best known as a resort of imperial tradition, but today its thriving economy is based mainly on industry. Even though the industrial sector has become increasingly diversified, textiles and clothing is still the town's main industry, giving employment to almost half its industrial labour force. While the spinning and weaving industry has been in decline, the knitting and clothing industry has been growing rapidly since the mid-sixties. This growth is best reflected in the Rua Tereza of Petrópolis, where hundreds of shops offer wholesalers, retailers and consumers a wide variety of knitted clothing. From here a network of production fans out, taking in not only capitalist enterprises, but also an unknown quantity of small domestic workshops, many of which are not registered.

The growth of this industry became very clear from

the interviews, in particular from the information given by the local machinery supplier, whose sales had increased considerably over the previous years. The rise in the number of people seeking her services in order to set up small businesses is particularly indicative of the expansion of domestic industry.

Attempts to quantify this growth were not very successful, mainly because official statistics only include legally established firms so that non-registered firms, generally domestic workshops, are left out. The scale of the problem is enormous. As mentioned before, the Industrial Census of 1970 shows for the entire state of Rio de Janeiro a mere thirty knitting and twenty-five clothing firms with less than five persons employed. According to our respondents, there were hundreds of such small enterprises in Petrópolis alone. In order to build up a quantitative picture, at least of the legally established firms (generally medium or large-sized), a number of registers was consulted, some of which were specifically prepared for this research. They suggested that in 1977 there were around 260 legally established knitting and clothing firms in Petrópolis.[19] Unfortunately the sources, even if taken together, cannot provide data on changes over time in the number of firms and workers.[20]

Whatever the data problems, the town's knitted clothing production has undoubtedly expanded. This growth has to be seen as part of the general expansion of the country's clothing industry, which is due to two factors: the displacement of made-to-measure clothing and the increasing population. While the industry is protected from imports, the growth of the internal market has been somewhat restricted by the prevailing income distribution. This came out most clearly in the words of a manager of a large clothing firm who was not from Petrópolis but expressed a general concern:

> Low wages, and I'm not saying this as a rule of economic theory, are the most serious problem of the clothing branch in Brazil, because there just aren't enough buyers. Quite honestly, I think that the minimum wage is unrealistic.

> Someone who earns Cr$ 1100 isn't a consumer,
> he's a marginal; the distribution of income
> affects the clothing branch very seriously.

Nevertheless, the trend towards ready-made clothing
makes for room in the market. The fact that Petropolis
became a centre of knitted clothing is probably linked to
the establishment of a knitting machinery manufacturer in
the town.

The Background of Small Producers

The interviews suggest that the people setting up small
enterprises are by no means unsuccessful job seekers. Four
of the five small producers and three of the present
medium-sized producers had previously worked as wage
workers, but had abandoned their jobs because of the low
wages. Some left no doubt that 'if my wage had been
better, I wouldn't have given up my job.' Others added,
'there's nothing like running your own business.' Indeed,
desires to have one's own business, to have less rigid
working hours, or to be able to look after the children
during work seem to be important additional motives.

All producers confirmed that they earned more than
they could have done as employees, but the differences
varied. In any case, the two are not strictly comparable
since the greater income of the small producer may be due
to the additional hours worked or the labour of other
members of the family. This will be discussed in more
detail later.

In order to better understand why some workers strive
to set up their own business, we set out briefly what a
worker can expect, job- and income-wise, in the knitting
and clothing industry. According to interviews carried out
in the larger enterprises, a sewing machinist earns between
one and two minimum wages,[21] hardly enough to keep a
family alive. An operator of knitting machines (generally
men) earns between three and four minimum wages. Once
they have been trained to operate the sewing or knitting
machines (which takes about three months) the work is
monotonous and repetitive and offers few possibilities for

upward mobility within the firm. The number of supervisory posts is limited and turnover in these low. Managerial posts tend to be unattainable in any case, as they are most often occupied by the owners of the firms. The designers tend to be the best-paid employees (between ten and twenty minimum wages), but these jobs are unattainable for most shop floor workers; they are few, generally only one or two per firm and require a very special type of skill. It is in this context of low mobility within the firm that the desire to escape from the tight work routine and the low wages can be better understood.

Most workers in the knitting and clothing industry are female, and indeed women often play the crucial role in setting up the firm, as recognised by the men:

> Before, I had a taxi, but my wife was employee in one of the firms here. She knew what the job was all about so we decided to start up our own business. We managed to borrow some money and bought a knitting machine, a Singer sewing machine, and an overlock ... all second hand .... When I felt that the knitting business was taking off, I decided to sell my taxi and invested the money in machines...

The husband stressed that he only decided to give up his work as taxi driver after the business, which was based primarily on his wife's labour and knowledge, showed signs of succeeding.

Technology

One basic condition for the emergence of the large number of domestic workshops in this branch is the existence of a technology which is divisible and does not require large capital expenditures. The necessary investment, as of July 1977, was around Cr$ 55,000 (US$ 3600) covering the equipment listed in Table 11.

This investment can be considered low in relation to the investment necessary to establish oneself in other industrial branches, but it is high for someone who earns

67

TABLE 11   Cost of basic equipment for knitted clothing production

Type of equipment	Cost (Cr$ of 1977)
Knitting machine (manual)	25,680
Winder	5,500
Sewing machine	8,920
Overlock machine	13,250
Steam iron	1,500
Total	54,850

Source: Machinery supplier.

two minimum wages, even if the amount can be reduced through the purchase of second-hand machinery. In fact, few are able to start with a complete set of specialised machines; rather they buy a knitting machine with their savings or on hire purchase (through the machinery representative). They then look to other workshops for help in doing the other stages. To quote the main machinery supplier, 'this is what they generally do; they buy a small knitting machine, make a garment and then take it to their neighbour to have the edges oversewn on the overlock machine; they pay (the neighbour) Cr$ 3 to Cr$ 5 per garment, and the rest they do by hand. Once they've got a bit of money put by, they get an overlock machine and then things get better, because, as well as doing their own work, they can do it for others too.' Like this they gradually build up their own set of machinery, usually combining both new and second-hand equipment.

In the debate on technology and employment in less developed countries one repeatedly meets the call for 'appropriate technology'. The information collected in Petrópolis from the machinery supplier and during visits and interviews in the places of work suggests that the technology used there has three essential elements of appropriateness: it is relatively cheap, labour-intensive and usable on a small scale.[22] Also, the creativity of the producers makes it possible to use alternative methods of production without altering the product to any great degree. This includes the adaptations which the owners make to their equipment in order to reduce the number of machines necessary. The explanation of one small-scale producer serves as a good example of this adaptation, 'we carry out four operations with a machine that was designed to do only one ... for example, we didn't buy a machine for cutting and hemming. We simply extended the piece of metal which acts as a guide for the cloth, pass it through the overlock and use the edge of it to cut the thread.' Similarly, if they are unable to buy a steam iron or an industrial sewing machine, they make do with an ordinary iron and domestic sewing machine; even though these do not allow the same productivity, they do cater for the most immediate needs of the enterprise.

Once a complete set of equipment has been bought, it is possible to modernise and expand gradually. For example, hand-operated knitting machines can be replaced or complemented with motorised or even automatic machines. Table 12 compares these three types of machine with regard to price, number of machines per operator, efficiency of machine (output per 8 hours per machine), and productivity of labour (output per 8 hours per worker).

Table 12 does not compare three theoretical cases but three types of machines which are on sale and are currently being produced. Thus, for a small producer there is a real choice to be made between equipment of varying degrees of sophistication and labour requirement. The most conspicuous point in the comparison is that labour productivity on a manual machine is six times lower than that on a motorised machine and ten times lower than on an automatic one. How is it then that the producer with hand-operated machines is able to compete in the market? First, these machines are usually bought to start up a knitting firm, when the low cost of a machine matters most; once growth of the firm is underway, motorised or automatic machines are bought. Second, flexibility of

TABLE 12 Performance of knitting machines

Type of machine	Price (Cr$ of 1977)	Number of machines per worker	Machine efficiency	Labour productivity
Manual	25,680	1	15	15
Motorised	36,400	3	30	90
Automatic	74,200	5	30	150

Source: Machinery Supplier.

production very often outweighs productivity differentials or economies of scale. Third, the remaining disadvantages have to be compensated by longer working hours. This also holds true for any of the adaptations which are, in terms of efficiency or productivity, lower than in the case of specialised machines. Having encountered a whole range of appropriate technology in the knitting and clothing industry, one must ask what the probable future trends will be. According to information obtained at the International Textile Machinery Exhibition in São Paulo in 1977, technological development is unlikely to represent a threat to small firms in this type of production.

Know-how and Skill

The majority of the people who start up a small enterprise have a good knowledge of the production process. This is explained by the fact that they have previously been employees of knitting firms. This forms, without doubt, an important means of transfer of know-how from the large to the small firms. In four of the five domestic workshops studied, and three of the five medium-sized enterprises, the owner or his wife had acquired these skills during previous jobs as an employee. This pattern was confirmed by the yarn distributor: 'Normally when a person begins in this branch, he knows it beforehand from working in a factory, or at least somebody in the family does.'

The principal machinery supplier (the local dealer, not the manufacturer) also has an important part to play in the training of small-scale producers. She gives courses of up to thirty lessons to her clients, based on an instruction book, written by herself (Custodio, 1976). As well as teaching how to operate the knitting machines and make up the garments, this course provides some basics for the calculation of costs and the organisation of production. The supplier's help is not confined to formal lessons but she can be consulted at any time by her clients. In the markets of sewing and overlock machines she has two rivals who also offer free lessons; these are however more limited in duration and content. Obviously, the relative importance of machinery representatives as transmitters of know-how depends on the knowledge that the client already has. For instance, ex-employees need little help with the operation of machines, but may require assistance in other tasks such as maintenance. It is worth mentioning that no case was found of a small workshop receiving technical assistance from the firm for which it produced garments.

A further means of training and transfer of know-how is that of one small producer learning from another, whether it be a relation, neighbour or colleague. The extent of this diffusion of know-how within the domestic industry is difficult to ascertain since it is not done in any organised way but rather through informal conversations or contacts with other members of the branch. Finally, learning by doing was for all producers an important way of acquiring skill and know-how in the various tasks which are involved in keeping the enterprise going. Certainly lack of skill and know-how is rarely a problem in the domestic workshops. This statement, coming as no surprise to those who know the world of small-scale producers, needs emphasis since the labour of the small-scale sector is often seen as low-skilled.

In the specific case of the clothing industry, let us consider the case of the seamstress, its main occupation. In a large firm she generally makes only a certain part of a garment, which means that, in terms of necessary training time, a period of only three months is needed to reach average productivity. In the small-scale enterprise she generally makes the entire garment which requires a training time of eight months. In the words of the owner of a clandestine enterprise: 'Work routines in the small firm mean that she has to know how to do everything. In a big firm the worker doesn't learn this, but just completes a single operation. In the small ones it's different, we can't work like that.' Indeed, a diversity of skills is required from the worker in the small-scale firm, and in the majority of cases the owner knows about the entire production process, about designing, knitting, sewing and finishing. As already mentioned, this knowledge is gained in previous employment, through contacts with colleagues, through the machinery supplier, and through a continuous process of learning by doing.

Registration

Having set up an enterprise, the owner's most immediate problems are connected with his illegal status. With a few exceptions, all workshops seem to have a clandestine origin. There was a consensus amongst the respondents that 'with the production from one (manual knitting) machine alone there's no way you can afford to register ... to legalize your business and survive you need at least three machines.' A lower production was considered insufficient to carry the costs of registration and the subsequent social security and tax payments. We found 'living proof' of this in a producer who had only one manual knitting machine and who had registered immediately after setting up his enterprise. He was in a worse situation than the other small producers interviewed (who had not registered), and his desire to 'have everything in order' meant that accumulation was all the more difficult for him. As one of the other producers said, in the beginning, 'you have to avoid those payments if you want to get anywhere; if everybody stuck to the regulations, I reckon there wouldn't be many enterprises here.'

Of course, illegal operation means a risk and fear of being discovered by inspectors and possibly losing everything that has been built up. The interviews reveal the constant threat of inspection, but also show that the enforcement of the regulations is not equally strict in all years and depends on the individual inspector.

> Five years ago they toughened up on control. I think they were unreasonable because they didn't take into consideration whether with only two machines you could manage to cope with registration .... Instead of giving (the person caught) some advice and guidance they took his machines away, and on top of that fined him; like that they finished with his enterprise .... But there were exceptions. I was caught by two inspectors who let me explain my situation and only gave me a small fine; they were very decent with me. I even sent them a Christmas card at the end of the year!

An additional risk is being denounced by neighbours. Virtually all producers work from domestic premises and that can have problems because

> the machines are noisy; sometimes you can count on your neighbour (putting up with it) but other times you can't. After ten o'clock you can't work on the machines, you have to respect their peace and quiet .... The other problem is the voltage. When somebody uses a normal sewing machine around here, that disturbs the "novela" (television series). It interferes (with the picture) all the time. Imagine what it's like with an overlock, nobody can watch television (undisturbed)!

Credit and Raw Materials

One of the main difficulties in attaining a level of operation which warrants registration is the lack of working capital. A bank loan is for the small enterprises but an unlikely alternative. As one of the clandestine producers said, 'who's going to lend money to a firm that

73

doesn't (officially) exist?' In the absence of bank credit, they have to turn to personal loans at high interest rates.

For the same reason the small producer has difficulties in the purchase of raw material. The spinning mills only sell against invoice, and the one thing that the non-registered producer avoids is having his name and address in another firm's books. However, registration alone would not change much, because the spinning mills stipulate minimum quantities to their customers. Since the small producers can only acquire small amounts of yarn at a time, they have to buy from intermediaries. This results in their paying 25 to 30 per cent more than medium or large-sized firms, sometimes even 40 per cent when supplies of a particular type or colour run short. This disadvantage emerged very clearly from the interviews with producers of all sizes and was confirmed by the yarn dealer (intermediary); she added that since her small customers 'haven't got much working capital, I give them 15 to 20 days to pay. They make the garments, deliver them and from what they get they take off the price of the yarn .... When they pay me, at the same time they take away a new lot of yarn (to be paid for next time.)'[23]

Markets and Competition

The small producers work primarily for the shops in and around the Rua Tereza. Many of these shops are merely the sales counter of the medium-sized firms. The small workshops are linked to these firms through the supply of garments or even parts of garments made to order (a type of subcontracting). In this way the medium-sized firms try to cushion the problems of unstable demand and to increase their range of products. Some of the workshops in Petrópolis work exclusively to order for boutiques in Rio de Janeiro, but they seem to be the exception. Contrary to expectations, subcontracting is little used by the large firms, but is common within domestic industry, where the clandestine producer frequently uses the services of other domestic workshops. Finally, small workshops also sell direct to the consumer, but this is less common and used only as a supplementary source of income, since this outlet is too sporadic to guarantee survival.

The essential point to be made in relation to the market of the knitted clothing manufacturers of Petrópolis is that the medium-sized firms, together with the domestic workshops make up a 'sub-industry' while the large firms operate separately in a different market. The strength of the former lies in their ability to thrive on the changes in fashion and to respond to a very diffuse retailing network. This requires great flexibility in production, which is characterised by very small batches and diversification of products. The small and medium-sized enterprises are capable of constant changes in models, patterns and colours at short notice. According to one well established and influential owner in the Rua Tereza, 'If you want to sell knitted goods, you have to dress them up in a thousand different ways ... big firms can't cope with that. We, who work on a small scale, can manage all types of hooks and eyes, loops and fancy stitching.' This flexibility in responding to small orders of different types is one of the most important factors in the survival and growth of these producers.

Of course the large firms do not produce unfashionable garments, but they operate in more predictable markets, and above all, have different channels of marketing. They sell through representatives to all parts of Brazil and leave only 'left overs' to be sold in the shops of Petrópolis. In contrast, the medium-sized enterprises sell their garments (produced by themselves or by associated domestic workshops) over the sales counter in their factory or through their shops in the Rua Tereza. Since they sell direct to the consumer or retailer, their market is more regionalised. The retailers include shopkeepers, stall holders at fairs, street sellers or people who supplement their income by selling clothes to neighbours, friends and work colleagues.

It is difficult to clarify to what extent competition between enterprises of different size is also limited by different products, apart from the product differentiation mentioned above. The big firms apparently produce lighter garments all year round, while the others concentrate on heavier articles for the winter; but some manage to work with garments for both seasons, which indicates that this division of labour is by no means rigid. In fact, from a technological point of view, products of the large firms could be made by the medium or small firms and vice versa.[24]

To summarise, it appears that the medium-sized enterprises and the supplying small producers concentrate on those articles which are particularly prone to seasonal factors or changes in fashion and which are sold through a retailing system which requires such short-term flexibility that it is incompatible with the programming of production in large firms. This division, however, is not clear-cut, and it seems that in general, as several of the producers said, 'there's room for all and everyone in this market.'

Costs and Profits

We have already seen that the fate of the small producers is intimately linked to the medium-sized enterprises. This becomes most apparent when the latter have to react to a drop in sales by reducing production. In such cases their first line of cuts are orders to domestic workshops, rather than the dismissal of their own workers.

In an attempt to define the pressures which small workshops have to overcome in slack periods, Table 13 compares their production costs with those of medium-sized enterprises. Such cost comparisons are hazardous, because the small producers concern themselves with two figures only: the cost of the yarn for a garment and the price they can get for it. While they realise that the difference is not wholly profit, they are rarely concerned with breaking it down. Instead, they usually add to the cost of the yarn a rule of thumb margin assuming that this will cover other costs and allow for a profit. The margin (percentage) varies a little with the product, depending on the design, or finishing, or the intensity of demand. The figures in Table 13 are averages of the respective costs and profit figures given by medium and small producers for a variety of garments. While they have to be treated as approximations, they help to illustrate the conditions of the producers linked to the Rua Tereza.

TABLE 13   Cost comparison of medium and small-scale knitting enterprises

(percentages)

Production costs	Medium-sized enterprise	Small-scale enterprise
Raw material	50	65
Labour	25	
Overheads	25	35
Total	100 excluding profit	100 including profit

Source: Interviews with producers.

In the medium-sized enterprises, raw material accounts for about 50 per cent of production costs. The remaining 50 per cent is divided almost equally between labour costs (wages and social security payments) and overheads (wear and tear on machines, electricity, rent, taxes, etc.). Generally, profit margins are around 20 per cent in sales to the retailer and 50 per cent in sales direct to the consumer.

As the small workshops work primarily for the medium-sized firms, the selling price they can obtain tends to be levelled at the latter's costs of production. If it were higher, it would not be worth their while buying from the domestic workshops. However, the workshops pay on average 30 per cent more for raw materials, in this way it takes up an average of 65 per cent of their costs of production leaving only 35 per cent for labour, overheads and profit.

This is where the difference between the registered and clandestine workshops comes in. Social security and tax payments make up 20 per cent of production costs. The clandestine enterprise does not pay these, but if it is able to pass them on to the buyer, it will have a profit margin of at least 20 per cent. The problem is that this does not always happen, because of the strong competition and the pressure which can be applied by the firm to whom they sell. As a result, this margin of 20 per cent is sometimes absorbed by the firms they work for; these know not only the exact production costs of a garment (from their own experience as producers), but also know the illegal situation of the workshops. The loss of this margin would leave the workshops with only 15 per cent to cover labour, overheads and profit.

Let us suppose, by way of an example, that the yarn for a garment costs Cr$ 32.50. The garment should then sell for Cr$ 50.00, divided as follows:

	percentages	Cr$
raw material	65	32.50
social security and taxes	20	10.00
all other expenses and profit	15	7.50
total	100	50.00

When workshop owners manage to sell at Cr$ 50.00, there is a minimum profit of 20 per cent resulting from social security and taxes which are not paid. But supplying to the firms of the Rua Tereza, they may lose this margin, being left with a final price of Cr$ 40.00 (Cr$ 50.00 minus 20 per cent) and with only Cr$ 7.50 for all expenses (other than raw material) and profit.

Domestic workshops could increase their profit margin by selling direct to the retailer (from outside the town) or direct to the consumer; but access to this market is difficult, given the illegal work conditions and the absence of their own sales outlets.

The ups and downs of the branch and the small profit margins make accumulation very difficult and indeed virtually all respondents emphasised that many small producers failed and went out of business. It is equally clear that some have succeeded in accumulating the capital necessary to develop gradually into capitalist enterprises. Even though an exact number cannot be given, when talking about the development of the local knitting and clothing industry, the respondents reported a number of 'success stories'. Also, of the five medium-sized producers interviewed, four had begun as domestic workshops.

What are the factors which allowed small enterprises to expand? Obviously knowing the rules of the game and jumping at good opportunities are extremely important in a branch as erratic as the knitting and clothing industry. Another basic condition seems to lie in the utilisation of labour.

Labour Utilisation

A small producer cannot expand unless he is prepared to increase production through longer working hours and/or involving the whole family in the production process.

Production is often shared among parents, children and near relatives, with the men working on the knitting machines and the women on the sewing and overlock machines. The children help with simple tasks when they are small. 'I've got two daughters (10 and 11 years old) who help to unravel and rewind yarn and give a helping hand generally.' Older children can help with the more difficult tasks, freeing the mother or father for the external work of buying raw material (yarn) and delivering the finished products. As another domestic producer said, 'I don't have to pay my children a wage, so their labour is my profit.' Help from members of the family who have another job or who are retired is also important.

The work routine in these enterprises is hard; as the machinery supplier said, 'normal would be eight hours a day, but they work overtime, work all night long. One son works till ten at night (on the knitting machine), then someone else takes over till two in the morning or even till the following day.' In the words of a small producer, 'the work is tiring and if you don't work more than eight hours a day, it's no good. There's no breaks here, no Saturdays off, no holidays. Sometimes we even work on Sundays.' Another workshop owner added, 'When there's work you really have to put in extra hours, because there are also other times when there isn't much to do.'

For these reasons it is very difficult to make any comparisons between the income of a domestic workshop and that of an employee. As already hinted before the interviewees found that their domestic workshops gave them a total family income greater than their income earned as employees. They emphasised that their earnings were much more irregular but left no doubt that they were overall better off than they would be as employees. This does not, however, exclude the possibility that hourly income (taking into consideration all the extra hours worked and the entire family labour) could be less than the hourly wage of an employee. But this calculation is probably irrelevant for these families, since they can combine this work with other obligations such as housework, caring for children, or studying; the advantage of not being tied to the fixed timetable of employees seems to outweigh other disadvantages, even if it means working in total longer hours.

The family set-up also makes it easier to survive periods of insufficient work and conversely to increase the work force promptly when business picks up again. In such periods the family workforce is sometimes further increased with wage labour from outside the family. It was found that these workers have the same take-home pay as those in medium or large enterprises, but apart from the greater irregularity of work, they also forego the legal rights and benefits connected with having a signed work card (being registered).

Summary

The main point which comes out of this initial experience is the perspective in which small-scale production has to be seen. It seems erroneous to consider it primarily as a form of survival for people who cannot get employment in the larger enterprises. On the contrary, it becomes an alternative for some of the workers of these enterprises to escape the poverty which results from their low wages. What needs emphasising here is that the worker seeks access to his own means of production to improve his situation. The technological conditions in the knitting and clothing industry open up this route, but at the same time make for intensive competition, where survival and expansion are guaranteed only through increased work hours and/or the inclusion of family labour. This 'solution' is not open to all workers but it is an important factor in explaining the emergence of the small workshops.

Those small enterprises that manage to grow, seem to find room in the market as there is a demand for knitted clothing which is channelled through a very diffuse distribution network, which in turn calls for a flexible production network. Thus, this study gives an example of the small and medium producers having a comparative advantage due to their flexibility.

2.4 The Hammock Industry of Fortaleza

If the study of the knitting and clothing industry revealed such great activity hidden behind the curtain of official statistics, this was but little compared with the situation that awaited us in the hammock industry. This branch was studied in Fortaleza, capital of the state of Ceará, in the North East of Brazil. Fortaleza has been one of the fastest growing cities in the region and its population passed the one million mark in the mid-seventies, with approximately a quarter of its population being migrant (Moura and Coelho, 1975). Its urban poverty and lack of jobs are severe (Arias, 1978; SUDEC, 1973b), even though it is the third largest industrial centre of the North East.

Fortaleza's main industries are textiles and clothing; this is partly because the state of Ceará has a tradition in such production, but also because the regional planning agencies and development banks have provided strong incentives for the modernisation of existing firms or the establishment of new plants in these industries. These incentives do not include the production of hammocks, a branch which is totally abandoned and forgotton, but which gives work to many people. The official statistics do not bear witness to this, but our very first visit to a hammock factory revealed that an enormous workforce is involved. According to official records this factory had seven registered employees. On entering we counted fifteen workers and in the course of the interview, the owner told us that he employed several hundred people who worked for him in their own homes. Later on this enterprise turned out to be an extreme case, but our estimates still suggest that the real labour force is at least six times larger than indicated by the official statistics.[25] Let us have a brief look at these statistics.

Secondary Data

According to the Industrial Census of 1970, the hammock industry employed in the whole of Brazil some 1499 people, more than half of them in the state of Ceará (see Table 14).

TABLE 14 Enterprises and workers in the hammock industry of Brazil and Ceará, 1970

Type of enterprise	Number of enterprises		Number of workers	
	Brazil	Ceará	Brazil	Ceará
Enterprises with five or more workers	86	43	1205	781
Enterprises with less than five workers	138	26	294	67
Total	224	69	1499	848

Source: IBGE, Censo Industrial.

TABLE 15 Hammock makers in Brazil, Ceará and Fortaleza, 1970

	Brazil	Ceará	Fortaleza
Men	1251	636	368
Women	4827	1539	407
Total	6078	2175	775

Source: IBGE, Censo Industrial; data for Fortaleza are taken from special tabulations.

TABLE 16 Enterprises and workers in the hammock industry of Fortaleza, 1976

Type of enterprise	Number of enterprises	Number of workers
Enterprises with ten or more workers	19	788
Enterprises with less than ten workers	19	78
Total	38	866

Source: Ministry of Labour, '2/3 Survey', 1976. The hammock branch belongs to the textile industry (branch 106 of '2/3 survey') and its data are not published separately. Only through a detailed register of textile enterprises, provided by the Human Resources Department of SUDENE, was it possible to compute the above data for 1976.

The population census of 1970 shows a much larger number, that is, 6078 hammock makers in the whole of Brazil, including 2175 in Ceará and 775 in Fortaleza (see Table 15).

More recent data (1976) from the Minstry of Labour show 866 people working in this sector in Fortaleza (see Table 16).

These are the data on employment in the hammock industry which can be taken from official sources. However, as already stated, our experience in Fortaleza suggests that in reality the workforce is far larger, even in relation to the Population Census.[26]

An Initial View of the Working of the Hammock Industry

In order to understand why there is such a big discrepancy between reality and official employment statistics, especially those based on enterprise surveys, one needs to know how hammock production is organised. Only in the course of this study will it be possible to show how it works in detail, but the following diagram can be used as a starting point:

Production in capitalist enterprises based on wage labour	
Production in subcontracted domestic workshops based on family labour	Finishing of hammocks carried out by women, children and old people at home
Production in independent domestic workshops based on family labour	

Hammocks are produced in two types of enterprise: first, those based on wage labour, in other words, capitalist enterprises; second, those based on family labour, the domestic workshops. Both types distribute a part of the production, the finishing, to home-workers, mainly women, who do this in their own homes. In reality, the division between 'capitalist enterprise' and 'domestic workshops' is not a rigid one, because the latter also employ some wage workers. However, their owners are generally forced to engage themselves directly in the production process and their capacity to manage and supervise is thus severely limited.

Workers who do not enter official statistics can be found even within the capitalist enterprises. These enterprises are registered, given that their size no longer permits them to remain clandestine, but even so, they rarely register all the members of their labour force in order to reduce their labour costs. It was noted that the men are generally registered, whereas the women are often not. Another way of avoiding certain labour costs is the use of external labour; a large number of the hammocks sold by the bigger firms are not made in their own factories, but in domestic workshops. These are usually clandestine and work through a subcontracting system whereby the factory delivers the yarn, the workshop makes up the hammock, returns it to the factory and is paid for the labour in yarn or money.

There are also workshops that buy yarn, make a hammock and sell it themselves. It is rare for these independent workshops, or those which are part of the production network of the bigger enterprises, to be registered. The labour force of the workshops does not enter the statistical surveys, even though together they employ nearly as many as the big enterprises. This conclusion was reached from information given by various producers who estimated that, in the state of Ceará, the total hammock production of the workshops almost equals that of the registered capitalist enterprises.

The total labour force of the industry still has not been accounted for. The finishing of the hammock is not done in the factories or the workshops. Practically all enterprises, whether large or small, hand on this work either totally or in part. It is entirely manual and done at home, involves a large number of people from poor families, especially women, but also old people, children or those with physical or mental disabilities. It is believed that the size of this external labour force is greater than the total number of people working <u>within</u> the large and small enterprises. However, it is difficult to be more precise, since many of those involved in finishing do not work either constantly or regularly and the time spent in this work varies considerably according to the type of hammock.

The finishing of the luxury type is a delicate and laborious process, while the finishing of the standard hammock is much simpler. The workforce for certain types of luxury finish even takes in women living in the interior of the state of Ceará who work, through an intermediary, for the enterprises of Fortaleza on the coast. There are families whose sole source of income lies in the finishing of hammocks, while others do this part-time in order to complement the family income.

For these reasons the workforce involved in hammock-making is very difficult to quantify and the very way in which the network operates means that only a small proportion of the total is included in official statistics. This recognition is not new and is confirmed in a study of artisans in Ceará carried out in 1962.

> Given the large number of production units (in Fortaleza) functioning in the form of domestic workshops, it is well-nigh impossible to estimate their numbers .... The industrial enterprises as such, involved in systematic production of hammocks, come to two or three at the most, while the others finance production in small domestic units or confine themselves to supplying yarn to the non-registered producers, who, partly for this reason, become subsidiaries of these enterprises, or dependent on those who can legally buy the raw material. (Rios, 1962, p.127)

In order to complement this picture, it is worth adding some earlier observations of a writer who tried in the fifties to give a quantitative account of the hammock industry (Cascudo, 1957):

> The Santo Antonio enterprise in Mossoró has 25 employees, but has between 600 and 700 out-workers .... It is not possible to estimate the number of people who work in hammock production and who earn money from it, some even using the spare time available after their main work. Information from all hammock producing areas of Brazil is unanimous in confirming the impossibility of calculating the number of private enterprises which, hidden away, are engaged in hammock production. (p.142)

This was written in 1957 and as already shown, is still valid today. It is this reality which essentially determined the research procedure described earlier (in section 2.1).

Most of the fieldwork was carried out in Fortaleza, which is the country's biggest centre of hammock production. The respondents included: eight domestic workshops with up to ten people working in them (seven workshops were clandestine) and eight capitalist enterprises (all registered)[27] with more than ten workers, none however had an internal workforce of more than 100. In the text, these domestic workshops and capitalist enterprises are often referred to as 'small' and 'large' respectively.

As well as the hammock producers, the following were also interviewed: ten people doing finishing work at home and/or distributing it to other people; a mechanic/machine salesman; a cotton yarn producer (whose main clientele were hammock enterprises) and three yarn sellers, one being a representative of a large spinning mill, one having a small yarn deposit, and the third (unregistered) going from one workshop to another buying and selling anything connected with hammocks. In addition, three enterprises in São Bento, state of Paraíba, were visited, in order to discuss with their owners some of the views put forward by the Fortaleza producers. The majority of these interviews were carried out in July 1978, with some additional ones made in November 1978.

The following account of the hammock industry is based primarily on these sources. First the process of production is explained, then follow sections on access to raw material, on competition and profit margins, forms of labour utilisation and finally an evaluation of the future of small-scale production in this branch.

The Production Process

The custom of sleeping in hammocks originates with the indigenous Indian population of Brazil; the first hammocks were made by indigenous Indian women. 'After manioc flour, the hammock was the next important element in the adaptation of the Portuguese conqueror', said Cascudo (1957)[28] in a study that describes the way in which, for four centuries, millions of Brazilians were born, lived, loved, died and were even buried in hammocks. Up to the present day the hammock is preferred to a bed by the majority of the population of the North and North East of Brazil.

From being initially a purely domestic product, the hammock became an exchange value produced by specialised artisans and their families. From the 1930s onwards[29] hammock production began on an industrial scale, that is, with wage labour, without however altering very much the existing technology. In fact, up to today the production process is almost craftsmanlike, compared with that in other textile branches. As we shall argue later, this is the main reason why big capital does not enter this branch.

The fieldwork in the hammock industry was carried out at the same time as some other work in the spinning and weaving industry. Coming out of a modern spinning and weaving mill and entering a typical hammock factory gives one the impression of going back in time, such is the similarity with a pre-industrial revolution workshop. The main stages of production are carried out manually, in both large and small enterprises; in some small workshops the only source of power available is human muscle. Work is based on the manual ability of the workforce, and in the words of one weaver 'energia feijão' (feijão, black beans, constitute a basic part of Brazilian diet).

The raw material used is thick cotton yarn and the quantity necessary varies according to the size of hammock desired, that is, whether it is for a child, or whether it is a single or double hammock. The cotton yarn reaches the enterprise wound on cones; it undergoes three different processes: dyeing, weaving and finishing.

<u>Dyeing</u>: the yarn must first of all be wound into large hanks, so that during the dyeing process the dye is distributed evenly. This is a simple but tiring operation; the yarn is wound onto a wooden frame (2m by 5m) which has along the vertical sides a series of pegs around which the yarn is wound. This long-winded operation is usually done by women or children, walking back and forth from one end of the frame to the other, holding a wooden baton through which the yarn passes and which serves as a guide.

When sufficient yarn has been wound, the hanks are gathered together to form one large one. This is then put into a large metal cauldron containing the dye and is left until the desired shade is obtained. Then the yarn is put on a line in the open air to dry. This job is very messy - the dye goes everywhere - and is usually done by men. The subsequent disentangling of the yarn is a time-consuming process.

<u>Weaving</u>: before beginning the actual weaving, it is necessary to prepare the warp (threads which run lengthwise) and the weft (those which run across), which when woven together form the 'cloth' of the hammock. The warp threads are wound onto the beam of the loom. Of the firms visited, only two used a mechanical process for this beaming. The weft thread is wound onto spools, called pirns, which are placed inside the shuttle, and propelled from side to side, weaving in and out of the warp threads and so forming the cloth. In the bigger enterprises, the winding onto pirns is mechanised, wheareas in the small firms it is done manually. This preparation for weaving is done by men and women.

The looms are wooden and operated manually. A loom has two foot pedals on which the weaver stands; using his body weight, he is able to change over the two sets of warp threads. His leg movements have to be coordinated with his arm movements; the shuttle is sent back and forth by pulling two ropes which are on the loom, at head level. Pulling the left-hand rope sends the shuttle to the right and vice versa. This work requires skill, especially when several different colours are being used. In all the firms visited, the looms were operated by men.

<u>Finishing</u>: this stage is sent out to women who do the work manually in their own homes. The woven cloth made in the factory has about 20 cm of loose threads at either end; these are plaited together in groups of about twelve to form a string; each string has a loop on the end. To strengthen these strings and loops, they are incorporated in two narrow bands which run the width of the hammock. These bands are woven by women on small, manually operated looms.

A cord is threaded through the loops, itself in loops which are about 60 cm long; these are gathered together at the end farthest from the cloth and bound to make one single large loop. This large loop (one at either end) is used for hanging the hammock and can be hooked over a special metal fixture in the wall, or some other projection. The cord used is bought ready-made by the small workshops, whereas the bigger ones have their own machines to produce it.

The final stage in the finishing of the hammock is the decorative fringe which runs along the two long sides. This may be very simple, a series of interlinking knots, or may be an intricate and beautiful lace-work fringe which takes several days to produce. The high quality of the fringe is one of the things which distinguishes a luxury hammock from a standard version.

In conclusion, it can be said that up to this day hammocks are made manually in Ceará with a few exceptions in the preparation for weaving. The question of whether this process will change technologically is discussed later. It is worth noting that the initial investment in equipment to set up a workshop is small. The loom costs between Cr$ 5000 and Cr$ 6000, together with the accessories (metal combs and shuttles).[30] To set up a small workshop in the backyard with three looms requires approximately Cr$ 20,000 for equipment. This is little compared with the minimum investment in other branches of manufacturing, though not necessarily little for those who want to enter the branch.

Access to Raw Material

The key to understanding the working of the hammock industry is the raw material and its financing. The bigger enterprises are supplied directly by the cotton spinning industry; this is not possible for the smaller workshops. Their first difficulty is that they are not registered and are therefore unable to buy direct; they buy from the larger hammock enterprises or other intermediaries (e.g. a yarn deposit) and therefore pay more for their raw material.

The main problem of a workshop is obtaining working capital to buy the raw material. The cost of yarn figures large in the total production cost; in the case of an ordinary hammock it may be as much as 75 per cent. Even a small workshop with three looms and a daily production of thirty hammocks needs at least a working capital of Cr$ 90,000 in order to keep going, that is, buy the yarn, make it up into hammocks and sell them. It is difficult for the small producer to accumulate this capital. Not being able to buy his own yarn, he has to turn to the bigger enterprises who give him, for example, 300 kg, on condition that he give it back made up into hammocks.[31] In this way, the owner of the yarn pays only for the labour, either in money or in yarn. This payment is less than the profit of a small independent producer and makes it difficult to save anything and consequently, to get out of the rut.[32]

But even for those who work independently, raw material is still the main problem. First, the small producer pays between Cr$ 6 and Cr$ 8 more than the large producer per kg of yarn. Second, he is more vulnerable to frequent price changes, which in turn make his production irregular. When the price rises, his working capital, which is already stretched, is reduced by the amount of the price increase. On top of this, it is very hard to pass on the increase to clients; the bigger enterprises generally keep a stock of yarn or finished articles and in this way can maintain the lower price for some time after an increase. But the small producer is unable to keep a stock of raw material or finished products; he needs to sell quickly what he produces, in order that his family and/or workshop survives. The end result is that he has, for a time, to produce with the increased cost, but sell at the old, lower price. This is exactly what forces many producers into extinction.

In fact, a point which recurred in many interviews was the extent to which the most recent price rises contributed to the closing down of many workshops. Some respondents estimated that half the workshops had ceased functioning (in July 1978); they put this down to the fact that the price of yarn rose from Cr$ 30 per kg in January to a surprising Cr$ 50 in July, which produced one of the biggest crises in the hammock sector of Ceará of the last few years.

Two important reasons for the increasing price of yarn were found. One was linked to the manœuvres of a large textile enterprise from the South of Brazil. This enterprise started up, with fiscal incentives from SUDENE, a new spinning mill in the North East, using spinning machines which are the world's very latest development in yarn spinning technology, called OPENEND. In comparison with a conventional spinning mill, OPENEND allows a reduction of the workforce by 50 per cent and makes it possible to use the waste products (of cotton processing or of knitting and clothing factories). This is a considerably cheaper raw material than pure raw cotton fibres. In this way, on entering the market this mill was able to sell thick cotton yarn for less than the then market price, which forced other mills to abandon this particular line or even shut down. Having reduced the number of producers in this way, the enterprise now dominates the thick cotton yarn market and dictates the prices.[33]

The spinning mill in question obtains the waste products from other textile factories of the group, which is one of the biggest and most powerful textile groups in the country.   According to one representative of the enterprise, this access to waste products gives them advantages over all other competitors. However, such raw material produces a weaker yarn which means that the hammock will be less hard-wearing. On the other hand what counts in the yarn market, according to the manager of another spinning mill, is less the quality than the price and the length of credit time given. In any case, hammock producers only benefited from lower prices when the new spinning mill entered the market. As other mills were unable to equal these low prices, they were obliged to withdraw from the market, so that competition lessened considerably. According to various respondents this factor contributed to a later rapid rise in yarn prices.

The second reason given for the high price of yarn was the export policy of the government. The export incentives led to an increase in cotton exports and therefore produced a scarcity of yarn in the internal market, which also led to a price rise. This meant that, in the hammock industry, many firms were unable to maintain their level of production, because they did not have the working capital available to obtain the raw material they needed. Both large and small firms were affected, but since the small ones were unable to hold a stock, this problem hit them even harder.

To sum up, the ups and downs of the small producers are directly linked to factors beyond their control, and even outside the hammock industry altogether. They depend on the supply of raw material, the thick yarn, whose availability and price is manipulated by the manœuvres of big companies and the government.

Markets, Competition and Profit Margins

One question we kept returning to was why the small producers cannot raise the price of the hammocks more quickly, concurrent with the price-rises of the yarn. The answer lies in the cut-throat competition which reigns in the market, or in the words of a hammock producer, 'there's no unity in this thing, there's no cooperation, there's nothing, it's every man for himself.' Competition is greatest in the standard hammock market where profit margins are lowest, whereas in the market of luxury hammocks the competition is a good deal less. In what follows, the different markets are explored and the implications for the profit margins of the workshops and capitalist enterprises are examined.

The bigger and more important market is that of the standard hammock, bought by the people of the North and North East. Based on information given by the producers themselves, it was calculated that 90 per cent of the population of the North of Brazil sleeps in hammocks, and also the majority of the population in the states of Maranhão, Piauí, Ceará, Rio Grande do Norte, and Paraíba. In the other states of the North East and some parts of the Centre West region, the hammock is also used, though to a lesser degree. Without doubt, the market is enormous, considering that the population of the states where it is most used (Amazonas and neighbouring territories, Pará, Maranhão, Piauí, Ceará, Rio Grande do Norte and Paraíba) accounts for some 21 million people alone.

Since the hammock is a basic necessity, one would expect the market to be increasing with the rapidly growing population of the North and North East. But the low-income level of the majority of the population has, perhaps, limited the market for standard hammocks. To quote one of the interviewees:

> I reckon that consumption's gone down because buying power's been reduced. If the harvest's poor then no-one buys a new hammock. They're already sleeping on straw in the North. Some shops around here are selling just end-loops and people are mending their own hammocks (because they don't have the money to buy new ones).

A solution for some hammock producers is to make the luxury hammock; here the principal markets are the local trade (which sells to tourists or to the few local rich), the Centre South and the foreign markets of Western Europe and North America. Generalising from the research sample, the market is not divided between small and large producers according to the type of hammock produced. Of the eight workshops in the sample, six made the standard hammock, and two the more expensive or luxury hammock. Of the eight bigger producers, two made the luxury hammock, four the standard hammock, and two made both.

There is a certain division of the market between small and large producers according to region. The main market of the large producers is the North, which accounts for at least 70 per cent of their sales, especially of the standard hammock; their second largest market is the North East. In these markets they sell to wholesalers and to big shops. In contrast, the small enterprises have as their main market Fortaleza or the state of Ceará. This applies to the domestic workshops and the smaller capitalist enterprises.

Let us now examine the marketing of the domestic workshops in some detail. Of the eight workshops, three work directly for large producers, and two do this only when they cannot get yarn any other way. The others work independently. They sell locally, mostly to small shops, the stall-holders of the Central Market, and people who buy in Fortaleza and resell in the markets of the interior. Their profit margin is between 5 and 15 per cent, generally 10 per cent. Selling directly to the consumer, profit can be 20 or 30 per cent, but few sales are made in this way. Table 17 provides an example of production costs and profit in a standard hammock produced in an independent small enterprise.

TABLE 17 Costs and profit in small hammock enterprise

(in Cr$ of 1978)

1.5 kg of yarn (no.8)	75
labour	30
= costs of production	105
+ profit of 10 per cent	10
= selling price	115

What does a profit of Cr$ 10 on every hammock mean in terms of monthly earnings? The direct question, 'How much do you earn per month?' is difficult for the interviewee to answer because he never works it out. First, profit varies greatly; second, family and firm are the same thing, money coming from the firm is used to buy yarn, rice or medicaments – in other words, everything comes out of the same purse. It is better to try to get an answer to this question indirectly. A workshop with three looms can produce on average thirty hammocks a day, or 150 a week, or 600 per month.[34] Six hundred hammocks means a profit of Cr$ 6000 per month, so long as no problems arise with the yarn or the sales. Whose work and remuneration is included in this profit? The workshop owners only calculate two items in their costs: raw material and labour; other costs, such as wear and tear on a loom, electricity etc., are not taken into account and indeed are at a minimum in hammock production, because the equipment is simple and most operations are manual.

The cost of yarn is easy to calculate, but it is difficult to know exactly what is included in the labour costs. In general, the owner does not include his own work or that of his wife or children, unless they are grown-up children working full-time in the workshop. So what they call 'profit' is, in part, the remuneration of family labour. Of the four independent producers interviewed who made the standard hammock, three gave Cr$ 30 per hammock as their labour costs, and Cr$ 10 as their average profit. The fourth case is an interesting one; the owner calculated only Cr$ 20 for labour, but worked with a higher profit margin, Cr$ 15 to Cr$ 20. Seven people worked in the workshop and, with one exception, they were all members of the family, including two sisters of the owner, who were mentally retarded. It was understood that the owner did not pay them a wage, but was responsible for their welfare, which had to come out of the 'profit'. This is just one example which shows that 'profit' is relative in a family workshop which might productively employ people who would not be able to find formal employment.

At the beginning it was thought that the registered workshop owner saw the clandestine producers as damaging to business, but as he himself does not register his labour (mainly family labour), the fact that the other small producers are not registered does not bother him. What does worry him is that some workshops are sometimes obliged to sell at or below cost price: 'Come Friday, he needs the money, so he takes a hammock to the market and sells it below cost price, there are buyers, stall-holders, who make a living just out of that.'

This was confirmed by one of the workshop owners: 'This week, these hammocks which cost me Cr\$ 105 (yarn and labour), I sold them for Cr\$ 90. - And so you made a loss? - Well, I needed yarn to work and so that I didn't have to halt production, I sold for Cr\$ 90.' It is the shortage of working capital which can force the small producer to sell quickly, at a determined moment, either because he needs the money for the purchase of yarn or possibly to cover family expenses. Unable to wait, he has to accept any price, even if it does not fully cover the labour that went into the production of the hammock. It is clear that in a market where there is already considerable competition, such practices exert a further downward pressure on profit levels.

The worst 'market' for the small producer is where he works solely for the larger enterprises in a subcontracting system. In such cases, the profit on a standard hammock is only Cr\$ 5. These subcontracting relationships will be examined in detail later.

The profit margin of 10 per cent for the independent workshops must be compared with that of 20 to 30 per cent for the large enterprises (selling outside Fortaleza and Ceará). Their costs and profits for a standard hammock are as shown in Table 18.

The production costs are practically the same as those of a workshop. On the one hand, the larger registered enterprise has higher labour costs,[35] mainly because of the social security payments of those employees who are registered. On the other hand, the yarn costs the bigger enterprise between Cr\$ 6 and Cr\$ 8 less, which, in a hammock using 1.5 kg of yarn, gives him an advantage of Cr\$ 10.[36] The profit of the big producer is a good deal more, mainly because he sells ouside the highly

TABLE 18 Costs and profit in large hammock enterprise

(in Cr$ of 1978)

1.5 kg of yarn (no.8)	65
labour	40
= costs of production	105
+ profit of 25 per cent	26
= selling price	131

competitivie market of Fortaleza and Ceará, that is, he sells to the North and other states of the North East or Centre West. This does not necessarily mean that these markets are easy.[37]

For the independent workshop there is one way to escape the strong competition in the local market; that is, to make the luxury type of hammock. An interview with someone who did so showed that his profit margin (over production costs) was twice that of another producer who made the standard hammock. The evidence of this respondent was confirmed by another luxury hammock producer, who had already expanded beyond a domestic workshop:

> I tried making a hammock like the others, but it was no good. So I started to find out about the possibility of making a better hammock, better finished, to see if I could get away from the tough competition here in Fortaleza. There are people who sometimes sell without a profit and damage the other producers. I wanted to get out of this mess, make a better-made hammock of a higher quality. I found there was a market, and that I could dictate the price and not the buyer, which never happened before; in Fortaleza it's usually the buyer who decides the price.

The investment in equipment for a luxury hammock is no greater than for a standard hammock,[38] but the profit is bigger. The obvious question is why more workshops do not make the changeover to the better quality product. Unfortunately, this was not asked in the interviews, because the question only became obvious afterwards during the comparisons of costs and profits of various producers.

Certainly the luxury hammock requires greater technical knowledge, and can therefore only be produced by someone who already has a certain amount of experience in production. But the main reason is thought to be the lack of working capital. First, the luxury hammock needs more and better quality yarn. Second, it takes longer to produce, because it passes through more hands, especially at the finishing stage, and so the capital is bound up for longer.[39] There is a further difficulty if the luxury hammock is to have fast colours. This cannot be achieved in the simple home process described earlier, but requires a high investment in equipment. Finally, it should be mentioned that between the extremes of luxury and standard hammocks exists a medium quality which makes the picture a little more complicated than would appear in this study.

In summary, the main product is the standard hammock made by both small and large enterprises. The small producers who do not have the working capital to buy raw materials can only work for the large ones. The only outlet of the small independent producers is Fortaleza, where the market is highly competitive, thus reducing the profit margin to half that obtained by the bigger firms. These bigger firms sell ouside Fortaleza and Ceará, in the other states of the North and North East. The luxury hammock market is less competitive and covers the whole of Brazil and abroad.

Labour Utilisation

The degree and type of labour utilisation is a direct result of the factors already analysed, that is, the production process and its organisation, the availability and price of raw material, and the high degree of competition in the market. These are the factors which determine the quantity and quality of employment generated in the branch, together with two general factors; the abundance of labour in the North East, and the political conditions, especially the current labour legislation and the complete absence of workers' organisations.

The diagram gives the labour categories which need to be considered, according to type of enterprise.

Type of enterprise	Internal labour force		External labour force	
Capitalist enterprise	Wage labour		Home workers	Labour of subcontracted workshops
Domestic workshop	Family labour	Wage labour	Home workers	–

As already discussed at the beginning of this study, the official statistics only take into account the internal labour force of the capitalist enterprises, and of this only a part. The internal labour force will be examined below then the external part, which includes the labour force of those subcontracted workshops and those homeworkers who do the finishing process.

Internal labour force. The basic fact of the labour market of Ceará is the great abundance of labour; in fact, the North East constitutes the biggest industrial reserve army of Latin America, in spite of the massive migration to industrialised states in the Centre South and to the states of the agricultural frontier.

Recently the hammock branch has created its own reserve labour as a result of the crisis it is undergoing. None of the producers interviewed, whether large or small, mentioned a shortage of labour; on the contrary, there are always people seeking work. The availablity of labour is so great that the enterprises do not need to train their workers; they only accept workers who already have some experience of the branch. There was a time, however, when they had to train people.

The key occupation is that of the weaver. To learn the technique and reach average production takes about two months. Other tasks are easier to learn. All training is done on the job, there are no courses on hammock production offered by private or public organisations.

Given that it is possible to find experienced workers and that labour turnover is high in the majority of firms whether large or small, there is no incentive for firms to invest in training. In the case of registered workers this is very much linked to current labour legislation. High turnover was a constant feature in the research; it was also found in the other branches investigated. The pattern is repeated: the guarantee fund (FGTS)[40] makes it easy to dismiss the worker when the firm wants to; at the same time it invites workers to provoke their own dismissal in order to receive their guarantee fund. In the case of hammock production it is difficult to quantify turnover, even though data are available on the length of service of employees.

As can be seen from Table 19, one-third of the workers has a length of service record of less than six months, and approximately one-half has less than one year, which indicates high turnover. But according to various respondents, it is quite common for a worker to hand in his notice and leave in order to take out his fund money, only to join again a short while afterwards. So a worker may have been working for many years in a firm, but according to the information supplied to the government has only been working for a short time. This makes it very difficult to have a more exact idea about labour turnover of registered workers and about the differences between firms which, it is thought, are not small.

Amongst non-registered workers, the instability also seems high. 'It's normal (the turnover) in hammock production. Today you've got ten weavers; in sixty days time you've only got one or two of them left. Others have

101

TABLE 19 Length of service of registered workers in the hammock industry

Length of service	Weavers	Other workers
		(percentages)
Less than 6 months	30	38
6–11 months	17	18
12–23 months	26	19
2–3 years	19	18
4–5 years	7	7
6 years and more	1	–
Total	100	100

Source: Ministry of Labour, '2/3 Survey', Register of Employees, April 1977. Data refer to five of the registered enterprises included in the sample and within these enterprises only refer to those workers who are registered. All firms had been in operation for more than six years.

already replaced them. People who aren't registered, they're always on the move', said the owner of a firm which has eighteen employees. The same is happening with the workers in the small firms: 'How long have your two weavers been with you?' 'They're new. Not even two months. They come and go. Work here and there. They never work for a whole year, at the most three to five months.' This quote represents well the observations of the other workshop owners who have more than one worker from outside the family. Why this high turnover? It is believed that low wages are at the root of it, as in the case of the registered workers who take out their guarantee fund in order to make up their income. The non-registered workers are prepared to change work-place or take up other employment wherever they have the chance to earn a little more, even if it is only for a short time. 'They leave one job for even the smallest rise in the next one', said one of the small workshop owners.

What the respondents did not say was that in many cases the workers are obliged to move because one week there is yarn and the next there is not, resulting in no work. But these aspects of instability in production and its implications for employment will be discussed later. It is worth noting that mobility exists between large firms, between small ones, and between the two.

Some producers explained the turnover by the lack of a sense of responsibility in the workers and explained absenteeism in the same way. 'He doesn't turn up on Monday or on Tuesday. On Wednesday he comes with a doctor's certificate, ill. I know what's wrong with him: hangover. Why should I pay him, knowing there's nothing wrong with him? It's a serious business.' (The owner of a firm with thirty-five workers.) It is interesting to note that the employer who spoke worst of his workers had been a car worker in São Paulo for eleven years. He now has sixteen employees. 'It's like I say, they don't turn up for work, they don't have the same sense of responsibility as they have in the South (São Paulo); I used to work in the South .... Here they often don't turn up. The more they've got, the more they stay away. If one week they earn a bit more, then you can bet that they won't turn up the following Monday.'

We do not have other evidence that there really exists a 'backward sloping labour supply curve' (the more you earn, the less you work) and we do not believe that the problem of hangover is specific to hammock production. In fact, some employers said they had no problem with absenteeism and had obviously imposed greater discipline; for example, they quickly dismissed those who were away too often. Absenteeism seemed to be more serious among non-registered workers.

Wages are low in the hammock factories. However, they are not lower than in comparable occupations in large spinning, weaving or clothing firms, and indeed it would be difficult, given the low levels in these industries. The minimum wage in Fortaleza is Cr$ 1111 per month[41] and no worker in the hammock industry earns more than two minimum wages. It is the weavers who earn most. They are all on piece-work and earn between Cr$ 300 and Cr$ 500 per week, the average being Cr$ 400 on the basis of 44 to 48 hours a week. There is no difference between the money wage in the capitalist enterprises and the workshops; the difference is that most weavers in the capitalist firms are registered and have certain legal rights, while in the clandestine workshops they have no protection whatsoever.

The rest of the workers earn less, about one minimum wage. Those who are registered are declared as earning one minimum wage but in fact, they are on piece rates, too. In order to calculate the piece rate, the boss divides the minimum wage by the amount of work he considers reasonable. 'I count how many hammocks they have to make to earn that wage. Anyone who produces more, earns more'; but there are those who do not even earn a minimum wage, especially women. One job which is not paid piece rates is that of the day workers who carry loads inside and outside the factory. This is done by men and they are paid one minimum wage.

Except for weavers, it is difficult to compare wages in the capitalist firms and the workshops, since in the latter these other jobs are generally done by members of the family. For grown-up children and relations, the remuneration is not all in the form of a direct wage, but also through board and lodging. These family ties make it difficult to compare wages. The owner, his wife and children do not receive a wage; as we have already seen, their work is not fully taken into account in a calculation of the labour costs. On the one hand it can be considered non-remunerated or under-remunerated labour, even in relation to the low wages of the capitalist firms. On the other hand, if the profit from the workshop is bigger than what they could earn together as wage-earners, then one could say they earn well. But in this case one should also ask whether the owner has an adequate return on the capital invested in his workshop.

<u>External labour force - homeworkers.</u> All the capitalist enterprises use homeworkers for the finishing of hammocks; this system is also used on a smaller scale by workshops. In total, this external labour is larger than the work force inside the enterprises. It is almost impossible to quantify the external labour force, because the interviewees themselves do not know. This is because they often use intermediaries who pass the work on, and because many of the people involved only work part-time. The owners were always asked 'if everyone involved in finishing had to work here in the factory, do you know how many people you would need?' A typical reply was 'no idea at all. But I do know we wouldn't survive economically, nor would they all fit in here.'

The more work that goes into the finishing, the better the hammock. On a standard hammock the finishing is much less than on a luxury hammock, but always involves more people than the previous stages of dyeing and weaving. More specifically, the following jobs are given to out-workers: the making of the plaited strings, the strengthening bands and the fringe. (The threading through of the cords and the making of the loop for hanging are often done within the enterprise.)

There are two ways of organising external work: one is for the firm to distribute the made-up cloths directly to the finishers; the other is through intermediaries. A firm which works without an intermediary saves on her/his remuneration, but on the other hand has to administer this work, which is 'pretty complicated' as one producer said of his colleague who used the direct system: 'He wants to see everything there in the office. There come twenty or thirty women and their children into his office with finished hammocks. He thinks it's good business, but it's really difficult to keep track of.'

The bigger firms generally work through inter-mediaries. Depending on the quantity and type of work, the made-up cloths and/or yarn are delivered to the intermediary's house, or s/he has to collect it at the factory.

Here is part of an interview on the production of fringes:

Can you please tell me how a fringe is made, how the work is distributed? - We don't make the fringe here, we have people who collect the yarn and distribute the work. When the completed fringes are returned, we pay the intermediary piece-rates. We don't know how much she pays her people.

Do you give out the yarn, and then take it off the price? - No, we give out the yarn and then pay per fringe. What we give out has been weighed, and then we check the weight of the completed fringes.

How many people do you have working for you, to your knowledge? - I really don't know, because here (internally) we only keep a register of the intermediaries. She comes and takes 5½ kilos of yarn. But I have no idea of how many women she has working for her.

But how many people come here to pick up the work? - We've got about 80, 100 or more. But each one of them has some five people working for her. So I reckon we've got at least 700 people just working with the fringes. They don't work full-time, only when they can.

But for your production, how many people would you need working full-time? - I reckon about 400 people. All over the Fortaleza area. Not just in the districts near here.

Do you think it's possible to earn a minimum wage doing this? - Just by making fringes it would be difficult, because it's a time-consuming thing, crochet takes a long time. There's one family whose only source of income comes from making the fringes, two elderly woman, and they don't make that much, on average about Cr$ 600-700 (the two women together, in one month).

One person working at this for eight hours a day can earn how much? - Maybe Cr$ 600. One of my fringe-makers manages Cr$ 1500 or Cr$ 1600, but her whole family helps.

> Are there registered people who do this? –
> Very few. There's a lot in the hammock world
> that doesn't get registered. As I say, we've got
> a big pay-sheet here, but in the official
> accounts we pay out little.

This extract is from an interview with a luxury
hammock producer; he produces seventy hammocks a day,
with only fifteen people working <u>in</u> the factory. It is
possible that he exaggerated when he spoke of 700 people
working for him from home, but even if half that number is
nearer the truth, then the size of the hidden workforce is
still impressive.

Another bigger producer who uses crocheted fringes
has a network of female labour which reaches into the
interior of the state of Ceará. 'There are women who come
by train every fortnight, bringing in what's ready. The
"leader" (intermediary) pays the women right there in the
station, they organise everything there. Anyway, the best
fringes are made in the interior.'

This same producer has many fewer intermediaries,
even though his production is greater.

> We've got eight women who work as leaders. We
> give them the hammock cloths and the
> necessary yarn for the finishing. They give
> them out to the dozens of women under them.
> All our dealings are with these leaders, our
> accounts are with them. There's a daily
> collection of hammocks. Each of these leaders
> is responsible for only one or two types of work,
> and the hammock is never passed on from one
> leader to another. It leaves here, comes back
> here, and then goes out to another one. You
> have to do it like this, otherwise you'd never be
> able to check them.

Two of these leaders were interviewed. The first gave
out work to more than 100 women, and on entering the
poor district where she lives and works, one could see
women taking hammocks away for finishing. Also, women

107

and children arrived during the interview, delivering or collecting hammocks. From the information that the leader gave, it can be concluded that a woman working full-time can earn Cr$ 35 a day, or Cr$ 700-800 a month. But this is only an estimate so that a rough comparison can be made with the minimum wage of Cr$ 1111. In fact, there are women who only work for a few hours a day, others who work an eight-hour day, or have children to help. (The sum referred to is for a simple fringe, made completely manually, just a series of knots). The leader herself said that she earns about Cr$ 4000 per month with the help of her old man and two grandchildren. This woman was the 'star' of the enterprise and headed the biggest group of women.

The other leader gave out part of the work (the plaited strings), and the other part (the strengthening band) she did herself in her shed with the help of her daughter and the three young girls she employed. They earned Cr$ 200 a week. The leader herself earned Cr$ 2000 a month. She spoke very badly of other producers for whom she had already worked and who 'pay really badly'. Both leaders emphasised in the interview that in their long experience of that type of work (roughly twenty years) their present boss was the first to pay health insurance for them.

One of the largest hammock producers entrusted the entire finishing process to two intermediaries. Five of the women working for them were interviewed and, using the information given by them on payment per piece and time taken, it was possible to calculate that they earned between Cr$ 300 and Cr$ 600 per month, assuming they worked 180 hours per month. One of them was so chronically ill that she was only able to work at home. It is worth mentioning that, according to one of the intermediaries, 20 per cent of the homeworkers' wages is already accounted for each month in advances. He also drew attention to the fact that there is a high turnover in this workforce. This was confirmed by another respondent who gave out hammocks in his district for finishing: 'Is it always the same people working for you, or do they change? - There's a lot of change over. They don't stay long. If someone else is paying better, they go there. Even if it's very little more.' Considering the poor remuneration, this is not surprising.

The workshops also use this workforce; of the eight visited, only two completed the entire hammock. The rest gave the plaited strings and the fringe to others to make. Very simple fringes are not ordered, but bought from women with a stock of ready-made fringes, who regularly visit the workshops. As the production of the workshops is low, they do not generally use intermediaries to distribute the finishing, but arrange things directly with the women who do the work.

To sum up, it can be seen that the hammock industry employs a vast external labour force, made up of women, children and elderly people. The abundance of this labour force enables the hammock producers to pay wages below those of their internal labour. Many of these people would not be able to get formal employment and for them it is a means of survival. Clearly, the availability of this labour would be considerably reduced if there were a social security system. Its non-existence is an important facet of the labour market in an underdeveloped economy.

External labour force - subcontracting of workshops. The section of the labour force which remains to be analysed is that of the workshops who work directly for the capitalist enterprises. In one sense, these workshops can be considered with the independent ones, but in fact they are an extension of the production network of the bigger firms. As one of the small producers who works in this system said, 'The guy delivers the yarn and pays for each hammock we produce. But sometimes he himself isn't a producer. I'm working for a guy who's never made a hammock in his life.'

From our sample of eight workshops, three used to work exclusively in this system, and two others only when they had no other means of getting yarn. From the sample of eight capitalist firms, only one had a series of external workshops, certainly the firm to use this subcontracting system most in Fortaleza. Another firm had used it in the past, and the case of a third is uncertain; the owner said he did not use it, while others said that he did. According to various statements there are also firms who do not themselves produce at all, but simply distribute the raw material to workshops and then collect the finished hammocks. This type of yarn distributor did not fall into the sample.

From the point of view of the workshop owner, there is only one reason for him to enter the subcontracting system; he does not have the working capital to obtain the yarn. For the contractor the principal motive is 'he wants to knock down production costs, so he secretly sends the yarn to so and so who produces the hammock, and gets paid x for each one, and the first guy gains his labour. There's a lot of that going on.' In this way, the owner of the yarn does not pay taxes or social security payments, because the workshops are clandestine. As well as this he makes the most of the cheap labour of the workshop, cheap because he is again in part using non-remunerated family labour. The non-family labour earns the same as in an independent workshop.

According to our information, the firm which most uses subcontracted labour in Fortaleza, has 260 people working for it, excluding those who do the finishing at home. Of the 260, there are 100 working within the enterprise and 160 working outside in clandestine workshops. 'Look, if I pay a minimum wage, plus health insurance and social security, who am I going to be able to compete with?' said the owner, speaking of the external labour. One of his external producers was interviewed; he had seven looms, three of his own and four belonging to the contractor. The hammock cloths are made in the workshop and the finishing is distributed in the district. Of the total number of workers, only one was registered, the workshop owner; he was a registered employee of the contractor, but 'he never gave me a penny in wages, not a thing, everything comes out of here,' that is, the production of his workshop and its non-registered workers. 'But don't the inspectors know there's a workshop here? - Of course they know. - And so ? - They ask who the workshop produces for, and so we tell them we work for Mr. X. Seeing as they know Mr. X, they go there and sort things out with him.' It was clear that bribery is common practice. This was confirmed by another subcontracted producer interviewed: 'Since I work for Mr. X, I send them (the inspectors) to him.'

The case of the latter workshop owner illustrated another advantage which subcontracting offers the contractor. Since demand is irregular, external labour need only be used when there is a peak in demand. The interviewee had already been working for Mr. X for three years, but had spent several months without work. 'Taking the last 12 months, for example, how often was there no yarn? – I reckon that for 6 out of the 12 months he didn't send any yarn.' This small producer was not an employee of Mr. X in the same way as the other interviewee, and worked with his wife and four children. They also had two employees, though only when there was work, since, 'if we have to stop because there isn't any yarn, we can't afford to pay a wage when there's not work.' During the months when they did not get any yarn from Mr. X, the women of the family went round other factories to pick up any finishing work they could get.

It is very difficult for the small producer to get out of this system of subcontracting, because he does not have the capital to buy yarn and his low profit margin makes it difficult to accumulate the necessary capital. His profit is about Cr$ 5 per hammock, compared with Cr$ 10 or more in the case of an independent producer. For example, a workshop with three looms can make thirty hammocks a day, or 600 a month. This would give a profit of 600 times Cr$ 5, or Cr$ 3000 a month including the remuneration of the owner and his wife. 'Does working independently pay better than working for a factory? – Good Lord! I should say so. About three times more!' From the interviews with the independent owners it became clear that it is often only twice as much, but in any case, the aim of the small producer is to be independent. However, in the beginning, he does not have the working capital to be able to work independently. One of the interviewees (the third of the subcontracted producers) had only been working for two months. He considered himself lucky to have got the yarn from a large producer who, according to him, did not have the room to expand within the factory and wanted to help him.

It is thought that the number of independent

workshops is greater than those subcontracted. However, those who work independently, if unable to sell their hammocks, go to a large producer and exchange a hammock for raw material, in order to continue working. There the hammock is weighed and the small producer receives an equal amount of yarn in return. His labour is paid either in yarn, or in money. Obviously the price he gets for his work is very low, because he is in the weaker position, he needs the money and cannot wait. Anyway, this too is a type of subcontracting except that it only happens when the small producer is in need, which does not mean that it is not good business for the large producer; he gets the labour of the small one at a very low price.

The practice of exchanging hammocks for yarn is very common, according to practically all the interviewees, because often the small producer, on his way to becoming independent, is left without the necessary yarn to be able to keep working in a stable, continuous way. The large firm gives him the yarn, sometimes only in exchange for completed hammocks, and sometimes it 'lends' the yarn to the small producer on condition that he return a ready-made hammock. Like this, the small producer who tries to work independently, slips back into a type of subcontracted work. This was what happened to two workshops where we interviewed, the owners attempting to avoid halting production but not always succeeding.

Breaks in production caused by lack of yarn are a common occurrence in the hammock world. As we have seen, in the case of the subcontracted workshops this happens because they are the first to be hit by any reduction in the production of the big factories; and in the case of the independent workshops the problem is that often they do not have the working capital to be able to produce regularly. This instability in the hammock industry is also reflected in the high turnover of workshops. It is impossible to quantify this changeover, but it was mentioned by several producers. Even one of the men who distributed hammocks for finishing and a small yarn seller used to have small hammock workshops but had to abandon them.

Despite the risks involved producers were committed

to this branch and did not seem to be prepared to renounce it in favour of wage employment. Of the eight workshops, four were owned by ex-workers of the large factories. The other four had always worked on their own account and did not intend to change. This is explained by their desire to have their own business and the economic advantage it offers over wage employment. As already seen, the worker who earns most in a hammock factory is the weaver, with an average of Cr$ 1600. A workshop owner with three looms, who works directly for the bigger enterprises earns roughly Cr$ 3000 a month including his own remuneration and that of his wife. Even if they were both employees, they would not earn any more. A workshop owner with three looms who works independently earns about Cr$ 6000 a month. The instability of workshop production is not taken into consideration in this comparison, but in any case, being employed in a factory is not necessarily more stable.

The Future of Small-Scale Production

It remains to evaluate future developments. To begin with questions related to technology: is there a transfer of technology and know-how between the large and small producers which could benefit the latter? Of the subcontracted workshops included, only one worked with looms of the contractor (as well as its own looms); it should be remembered that the loom is a simple piece of machinery, with no secrets, and relatively easy to acquire. None of the three subcontracted workshops, nor the other small workshops received any technical assistance from the big firms. Taking together the eight workshops, there was a flow of know-how in the sense that four of the owners were ex-workers of big firms. The other four had learned everything within domestic industry from members of the family, neighbours or friends. It is worth noting that part of the workforce in the big firms learnt the job in the domestic workshop. Overall, the transfer of technology and know-how from large to small producers is not an important factor in explaining the development of small enterprises. Historically, the opposite is the case, since

113

the hammock industry developed on the basis of domestic industry, without substantially modifying its craftsman-like process of production up to this day.

It was surprising to find a branch of activity within the textile sector which had remained almost untouched by the rapid technological changes which have affected the world's cotton textile industry. How is it that the branch is technologically so backward? As far as is known, hammocks have never been produced by the countries which are the main technological innovators for the textile industry (England, Germany, Switzerland, USA, Japan). This is not to say that Brazil is incapable of developing its own machines, but within the country hammock production is concentrated in the states where labour is cheapest, giving little incentive to invest in the mechanisation of hammock production. This seems to be the most plausible explanation of present technological conditions; these are backward but at the same time appropriate to the needs of the region which is characterised by great underutilisation of labour.

In the future, what likely technological innovations will the producer have to face in dyeing, weaving and finishing? The most common way of dyeing is described in the section on the production process. It is a cheap method used by the majority of the big and small enterprises. It does not, however, give fast colours. There is one enterprise in Fortaleza which does industrial dyeing with fast colours for hammock factories. This process is much dearer, and requires investment in sophisticated equipment, which goes beyond the resources of a small producer. Even so, if demand changes in favour of fast colours, this in itself would not necessarily destroy the small producer because, instead of buying brute yarn, it could be bought ready-dyed, or sent to be dyed in the specialised factory. However this would tie up more working capital in the yarn and could present problems for the small producers.

The major technological challenge to be faced in the medium and long term is in weaving. When the interviews were made in July 1978, all the looms used in Ceará for hammock production were wooden and manually operated.

According to some respondents a piece of cloth woven with a mechanical or automatic loom would be inferior and would be unsuitable for a hammock. Others disagreed, saying that in the state of Paraíba there are already hammock factories using mechanical looms. As this question could assume great importance for the future of the hammock industry, it was examined in greater detail. Some factories using mechanical looms in São Bento in the state of Paraíba were visited. A further visit was also made to Fortaleza in November 1978 and it was noted that three firms had each just installed two mechanical looms as an experiment and one producer had even ordered two shuttleless looms, the latest development in weaving. An attempt was made, in interviews held in São Bento and Fortaleza with some of those producers, and a mechanic/loom salesman, to assess developments in weaving.

One thing is certain; the claim that a hammock cloth made on a mechanical loom is inferior to one made on a manual loom is a myth. With a mechanical loom it is possible to reduce labour costs in the weaving of a cloth from Cr\$ 9 to Cr\$ 3. Their hourly production is higher and also one weaver can look after two mechanical looms at once. The automatic loom allows one man to look after even more looms but it is unsuitable because of the thicker yarn used in hammock-making. All the mechanical looms seen were second-hand. The cost of a second-hand loom is Cr\$ 25,000 including accessories and installation, as compared with Cr\$ 5000 for a manual loom.

It is surprising that all the producers who had experience of mechanisation said that hammock firms with manually operated looms could continue competing in the market, for the following reasons. First, the investment necessary goes beyond just the cost of the new loom, because a mechanical loom does not work well with yarn prepared by hand. As a result, anyone who mechanises the weaving must also mechanise the preparation of the yarn for the weft and the warp. The high investment in equipment would therefore slow down mechanisation. Second, weaving is only one item in the total cost and the reduction in total production costs achieved through mechanical weaving is so small that it can hardly render manual weaving obsolete.

As far as the shuttleless looms were concerned, they were still not in operation. It is unlikely they will enter the hammock industry, given the high costs of investment - around Cr$ 500,000, including accessories and installation. The producer who had ordered these looms believed that in his case they were technically and economically viable, since he already used the better quality twisted yarn necessary for the smooth working of the loom but only worthwhile in the luxury hammock, his principal line of production. He declared that the shuttleless loom was not a good investment for standard hammock production, but even for luxury hammocks one wonders how he can amortise the high investment, unless he manages to massively increase (and sell) his output.

Two of the larger enterprises had a type of hammock made from ready-made cloths bought from weaving companies in São Paulo and Santa Catarina, in the South of Brazil. According to the producers this practice is, and will remain, limited to a small number of more sophisticated hammocks.

One stage of production which will not change is the finishing. Two old machines were seen, adapted to make simple fringes, but the end results were of poor quality, and the machines were not a solution in terms of mechanisation of the work. All those interviewed believed that finishing would continue to be a manual process, except for one producer. He thought mechanisation was possible, since there are operations conducted by textile machinery which are much more complicated than hammock finishing. According to him, the problem would be to find a mechanical engineer with an interest in hammock production and with the financial resources necessary. These technological innovations are unlikely to come about, since the textile machinery industry and mechanical engineering in general are concentrated in the Centre South, which does not show much interest in hammock production.

For the moment it must be concluded that present-day technology is not going to see radical changes in the near future and that the small hammock enterprise is not for the time being seriously threatened by technological change.

The next question is whether the product has a future. The standard hammock has a huge market in the North and North East. It is a basic necessity, and it is probable that the market will expand with the growing population, assuming that income levels can hardly fall any lower than they are already. One critical point could be the replacement of hammocks by beds, if the latter should become a status symbol. But the hammock offers many advantages in a tropical climate, as well as the fact that it is cheaper than a bed and takes up less space, since it can be 'rolled up' during the day. The luxury hammock has great possibilities for expansion in the markets of the Centre South and South Brazil and in Europe and North America, a market which is only just beginning to be explored.

As already shown, obtaining raw material and working capital is the main problem of the small producers, and a programme of support would have to concentrate on this stumbling block. This question will be discussed further in a later section on policy implications, but it should be said that the likelihood of government action being taken is not very great, considering that even the larger producers of hammocks are excluded from the industrial policy schemes for the region.

In fact, the focus on small producers in this study does not mean that for the larger enterprises it is all plain sailing. They are large firms when compared with the domestic workshops, but within the industrial structure of the country they are small, or at most, medium-sized. For example, a project to set up a new hammock factory (in the dimensions of existing factories) would not even qualify for financial and fiscal incentives from SUDENE because it would be too small in terms of the amount of resources requested. Thus hammock firms come up against certain problems of access to finance for machinery and raw material, since the main financing mechanisms for industrial investment are directed primarily towards very large companies and are thus highly conducive to further industrial concentration.

117

The Absence of Big Capital

Hammock production today is in fact the business of relatively small capitalists (and domestic workshops). Up to the end of the 1950s Fortaleza had four large spinning and weaving firms that also made hammocks. Three of these firms had a joint sales department which centralised the selling of standard hammocks, while the fourth operated alone in the luxury hammock market. The first three firms stopped production and the fourth reduced its number of hammock looms from eighty to thirty. Today, there is not a single big North Eastern or Brazilian financial group involved in the branch.[42] Why?

Generally, the absence of big capital in a line of production means tht the market is small and residual, or particularly volatile. This is not the case of the hammock industry which has a vast market within and outside the country. The fact that there are few economies of scale in hammock production would seem to explain only partly why big capital does not enter this industry. It is thought that there is an additional reason which is linked with the production of value and the extraction of surplus value.

Capital is a social relation, based on the extraction of surplus value from the direct producer, that is, the worker. Given a competitive situation, surplus value depends on two factors: labour productivity and the wage level. Labour productivity in the hammock branch has been low given the low level of mechanisation. Thus, in order to increase surplus value there was only one alternative – to lower or keep low the wages. Even though the official minimum wage has been low (and over the last years even below the cost of reproduction of labour power) lowering wages was only possible by by-passing the law; for example, registering somebody as earning a minimum wage, but paying less; not registering the worker at all in order to avoid social security payments; using external labour without registering it. This is difficult to organise in a large firm which needs a certain hierarchy, organisation and planning in order to function; these are difficult to construct within clandestine work relations. A small firm is much more efficient in this. For example, in the industry of embroidered clothing in Fortaleza, we noted that the biggest firms were gradually phasing out the use of external embroiderers because of problems of administration and planning, and were setting up an internal embroidery section. However, this only began to be economical with the introduction of a new industrial machine for embroidery. Our information on this branch is insufficient to reach a conclusion on this point, but it is worth remembering how the production process has developed historically under the regime of capital.

The historical tendency has been for capital first to draw together a large number of workers in the same place, then to divide the labour and perfect the work instruments for each operation, and finally to develop machines and to subordinate the worker to the machine. Technology has been one of the basic instruments in the politics of capitalist production, or, in other words, in the domination of the worker in the work-place, a basic requirement for increasing labour productivity.

Within the textile industry of Brazil, it was noticed that the spinning and weaving branch experienced rapid technological change over the last twenty years, reducing the possibility of the workers interfering in the speed of the process or in the quality of the product. This is reflected in a great reduction in the time needed to train a worker to operate a machine, which makes it easier to substitute one worker for another. Directors of modern spinning and weaving mills in the North East were interviewed and said that when recruiting workers, they preferred to employ those without previous experience in the textile industry. Within a short time the worker can be trained to carry out a small number of operations; control over his work becomes absolute, to a large extent exercised through the machine itself. The subordination of the worker in production has reached this stage in spinning and weaving, whose production process can be characterised by the following interrelated factors:

- use of machinery,

- conscious application of technological research,

119

- fragmentation of the work process, especially the division between manual and intellectual work,

- the ease with which a worker can be replaced.[43]

The hammock industry is far from reaching this stage. Part of it is organised under capitalist relations of production, but the production process itself is still artisanal, with each operation being controlled by the man and not by the machine. Big capital tends to enter lines of production where it can increase labour productivity through mechanisation, which also makes the problem of control and supervision easier. In branches where this is difficult, it could of course try to control the marketing, but in the hammock branch we found no indication of this. However, on the raw material side there have been significant changes as indicated earlier. The number of yarn suppliers has been reduced and one company has a dominant position in the yarn market. Whether this will lead to changes in the overall organisation of the hammock industry is hard to predict.

Annex: Estimates of Production and Labour Force

This annex contains some estimates of total production and total labour force of the hammock industry in 1978. It must be emphasised that these are only rough estimates and cannot be taken as 'data'. At best they give some indication of the order of magnitude of the branch.

Production. According to an expert on the cotton yarn market of the state of Ceará, the total yarn consumption of the hammock producers of Ceará reaches 500 to 600 tons per month. Assuming that the average weight of a hammock is 1.5 kg, monthly production would be between 330,000 and 400,000 hammocks. (Table 20 assumes 360,000). The informant could not give a figure for yarn consumption for the town of Fortaleza, but it is possible to reach an estimate of the number of hammocks produced. With the help of knowledgeable insiders, an estimate was made of the number of looms in registered enterprises in Fortaleza.[44] A total of 440 looms in operation was arrived at. Assuming that each loom produces on average ten hammocks per day for twenty-two days a month, this would give a monthly production of 96,800 hammocks, in the internal production of the registered enterprises alone. It is much more difficult to estimate the production of the clandestine sector. Based on the opinions of various respondents it would not seem exaggerated to put the total production of the clandestine enterprises at two-thirds the total production of the registered ones which would amount to 65,500 hammocks.[45] This would give a total production of 161,300 for Fortaleza, or roughly 160,000 hammocks per month.

Jaguaruana is the second biggest centre of hammock production in Ceará. In interviews with two producers of Jaguaruana, its monthly production was estimated to be 100,000 hammocks. Putting together these estimates one arrives at production figures for the state of Ceará as shown in Table 20.

TABLE 20 Hammock production in the state of Ceará, 1978

Fortaleza	160,000
Jaguaruana	100,000
Rest of Ceará	100,000
Total	360,000

According to two producers of São Bento in the state of Paraíba, monthly production there is around 80,000 hammocks and the total production of the state is 100,000 or more.

Fortaleza, Jaguaruana and São Bento are the principal centres for the production of hammocks in Brazil, but they are also produced in other states of the North East, especially in Rio Grande do Norte (town of Mossoró), Pernambuco (Timbaúba), and Piauí (Pedro II). It is very hard to estimate the production of the other states of the

121

North East, but it is thought unlikely that their total production would equal that of Ceará and Paraíba. As far as is known, there are no factories outside the North East.

Labour. An estimate of the number of workers in the hammock industry cannot be obtained through a survey of the enterprises for the reasons given in the first part of this study: the registers do not include clandestine firms[46] and the producers only give information on the internal workforce. Generally they are unable to estimate the external labour force, since the finishing stage is passed on via intermediaries, and since many finishers do not work full-time on this job.

For this reason, there is only an indirect way of estimating the numbers of workers involved; this is through the numbers of hammocks produced, based on the estimates given in the previous section. This can be but a rough estimate, since the work which goes into a hammock varies according to its size and type. To produce a standard hammock takes approximately a total of three man hours, while the luxury version may take two days or more. If one assumes (arbitrarily) that on average a hammock take six hours to make then the monthly production of Fortaleza of 160,000 hammocks would take 960,000 hours. Taking as a basis 180 hours per person per month, this would give 5333 people working full-time for the enterprises of Fortaleza. This would seem to be a conservative estimate.

If this number is compared with the 866 workers given by the 1976 Ministry of Labour Survey,[47] the most recent available source, it can be concluded that the true workforce is at least six times greater than the figure given in the official statistics.

Finally, it must be stressed that the methods used in these estimates are questionable and that the results should only be taken as a rough guide to the number of hammocks produced and the labour force involved in their production. The only justification for this procedure is the complete absence of other data and the necessity of having at least an idea of the order of magnitude of the branch examined in this study.

2.5 The Weaving Industry of Americana

The survival of the small producers examined in the third case study was under more serious threat, in particular from technological change. Carrying out the field work was somewhat easier than in the previous cases because the small producers operated in the open, being virtually all registered. This enabled us to make much more use of secondary data, which will be examined first in order to provide a quantitative picture of the place which the weaving industry of Americana occupies within the Brazilian textile industry. For the subsequent assessment of the small producers' growth constraints and the implications for employment and income, we will have to draw on our own information collected at the beginning of 1979. Americana is an industrial town in the interior of the state of São Paulo, located at a distance of 130 km from the capital city, São Paulo. It has a population of approximately 110,000 people.

The fieldwork covered twenty weaving firms and, in addition, interviews with two representatives of the local textile workers' union, two retired textile industrialists, and two machinery suppliers, one of them dealing in new, the other in second-hand machinery. The weaving firms were selected from a register of firms,[48] stratified by size. From these strata a selection was made on a random basis, except for two large international firms which were chosen to explore whether foreign ownership made a difference to the issues investigated. Sample attrition would have been very high in the case of small firms, if only those producers had been interviewed who were originally selected and still in business. Given a high turnover of small firms it became necessary to adjust the sample in the course of the fieldwork. In cases where firms had changed owners, the new owner was interviewed. If the selected producer was no longer in business (e.g. had gone bankrupt, moved on to a different industry, become an employee of another firm) an attempt was made to interview him, whenever he could be traced. Six of the twenty firms investigated had more than 100 workers and were independent, that is, were not subcontracted. The other fourteen producers were, or had been, subcontractors. They had less than 100 workers, twelve of these firms had less than ten workers.

Americana's Textile Industry in the Brazilian Context

Even though textiles is one of those industries which are more evenly distributed over the country, the state of São Paulo accounts for 55 per cent of Brazil's textile production, 54 per cent of employment and 62 per cent of the industry's wage bill (see Table 21).[49]

TABLE 21 Production, employment and wages in the textile industry of Brazil and state of São Paulo, 1975

	Brazil	State of São Paulo
Production (in Cr$ 1000)	60,833,060	33,485,683
Employment (no. of workers)	355,768	192,125
Wages (in Cr$ 1000)	4,624,373	2,833,763

Source: IBGE and FIESP (Federação de Indústrias do Estado de São Paulo); quoted from Sindicato da Indústria de Fiação e Tecelagem em Geral no Estado de São Paulo (1979). (In 1975, US$ 1.00 was Cr$ 8.12.)

Within the state of São Paulo, the capital city of São Paulo is the largest textile centre, while Americana is second in importance and therefore the main centre in the interior of the state (see Table 22).

The relative significance of Americana in the state's textile industry increases if the number of enterprises is taken as the yardstick. As can be seen from Table 23, Americana has approximately 600 textile enterprises which account for almost 30 per cent of the state's total. This reflects the great weight of small firms in Americana.

TABLE 22 Workers in the textile industry of the state of São Paulo according to location, 1975

	Number of workers	Percentage of total
Greater São Paulo	122,305	61.4
(capital city of São Paulo)	(91,470)	(45.9)
Interior or rest of state	76,958	38.6
(Americana)	(14,841)	(7.4)
Total	199,263	100

Source: Caixa Econômica Federal (CEF), Programa de Integração Social (PIS); quoted from Serviço Nacional de Aprendizagem Industrial (1978).

Indeed, this large number of small producers is one of Americana's major characteristics; another is that the majority of these enterprises operates as subcontractors, involved in the production of cloth. Locally they are known as 'façonistas' or said to work the system of 'fação' in which a parent firm delivers the yarn to a subcontractor, who turns it into cloth and returns it to the parent firm paid by the metre of woven material. Table 24 shows the number of independent and subcontracted enterprises in the state of São Paulo. (A producer is called 'independent' as opposed to 'subcontracted' if he buys his own raw material and sells his product on the market.) The very high percentage of subcontracted firms in Americana does not necessarily set it apart as an atypical textile centre, at least not in this state,[50] since a large number of the town's firms is subcontracted by firms from the capital city. Thus, Americana's industry should be conceived of as an extension of the capital's industry rather than being

TABLE 23 Distribution of enterprises in the textile industry of the state of São Paulo, according to registered capital and location, 1976

Location	up to Cr$ 100	101–500	501–1,000	1,001–5,000	5,001–10,000	10,001–20,000	20,001–50,000	50,000 +	Total
Americana	450	78	29	28	11	4	2	1	604
São Paulo (capital)	225	195	112	193	64	47	23	28	887
Other towns	257	80	35	90	32	16	19	9	538
Total	932	353	176	311	107	67	45	38	2029

Source: Sindicato da Indústria de Fiação e Tecelagem em Geral no Estado de São Paulo, Relação das Empresas Têxteis do Estado de São Paulo, 1976.

TABLE 24 Distribution of independent and subcontracted enterprises in the textile industry of the state of São Paulo according to location, 1976

Location	Independent	Subcontracted	Part independent/part subcontracted	Total
Americana	129	467	5	601
São Paulo (capital)	829	42	10	881
Other towns	324	213	3	540
Total	1282	722	18	2022

Source: Sindicato da Indústria de Fiação e Tecelagem em Geral no Estado de São Paulo, Relação das Empresas Têxteis do Estado de São Paulo, 1976.

127

TABLE 25 Independent and subcontracted firms in the textile industry of Americana according to size of firm, 1975

Type of firm	Size of firm according to number of workers								
	0-4	5-9	10-49	50-99	100-199	200-499	500+	Total
Independent	10	14	40	10	13	9	6	102
Subcontracted	281	93	80	5	-	-	-	459
Part-independent/ part-subcontracted	2	3	20	3	3	-	-	31
Total	293	110	140	18	16	9	6	592

Source: Universidade Estadual de Campinas, Cadastro Industrial da Sub-Região de Campinas 1975-76, Vol. 1.

128

TABLE 26 Workers in independent and subcontracted firms in the textile industry of Americana according to size of firm, 1975

Type of firm	Size of firm according to number of workers							
	0-4	5-9	10-49	50-99	100-199	200-499	500+	Total
Independent	9	94	119	704	1833	2791	4943	11293
Subcontracted	458	609	1238	296	-	-	-	2601
Part-independent/ part-subcontracted	5	22	543	118	437	-	-	1235
Total	472	725	2600	1228	2270	2791	4943	15129

Source: Universidade Estadual de Campinas, Cadastro Industrial da Sub-Região de Campinas 1975-76, Vol. 1.

contrasted with it as a separate centre.

Table 25, compiled from a different source, shows that in Americana the majority of the subcontracted enterprises is very small, with 62 per cent of them employing less than five workers and 81 per cent less than ten workers. What is even clearer is that very few small enterprises manage to be independent, namely only 3 per cent of the former and 6 per cent of the latter categories. Thus small is almost synonymous with subcontracted.

The distribution of the labour force over the various types of firms is given in Table 26. What stands out is that the independent firms, while only representing 17 per cent of the total number of firms, employ 75 per cent of the total labour force. Thus the importance of subcontracting is put into perspective. However, our own investigations suggest that the data underestimate the number of people working in subcontracted firms. To calculate the actual number of workers one would first have to include the owners of the small enterprises in the workforce as they are directly involved in the process of production. This is a significant omission, given the great number of small enterprises and the fact that they are often set up and owned by two or three persons who pool their resources and work together. Second, it can be assumed that some of the workers of the owners' families are not included in the statistics. Third, these enterprises rely heavily on young unskilled workers who are not always registered during their first few months of training on the job. Finally, the data on large and independent enterprises include administrative personnel whereas those on subcontractors do not; their entire clerical work is done by specialised agencies to which they pay a monthly fee. While all these additions are necessary to arrive at a correct interpretation of the data, they must not be exaggerated; the sum of these omissions would perhaps add another 1000 people to the workforce of small subcontracted enterprises.

All tables so far have been based on data for 1975 or 1976. Have there been any significant changes since then? The most recent data available are from December 1978, and are given in Table 27.[51] In comparison to the 1975/76

TABLE 27 Firms and workers in the textile industry of Americana according to size of firm, December 1978

| | Size of firm according to number of workers | | | | | | | |
	1-4	5-9	10-49	50-99	100-199	200-499	500+	Total
Firms	143	86	77	19	13	10	7	355
Workers	323	589	1703	1369	1920	2734	6057	14701

Source: Sindicato dos Trabalhadores na Indústria de Fiação e Tecelagem de Americana, Relação de Empresas e Número de Empregados com Base nas Guias de Recolhimento de Contribuição Assistencial, 1978.

data these show a much lower number of small enterprises. An examination of the data source, however, indicated that it underestimated the number of small producers.[52]

These doubts are further compounded by the data with which all enterprises have to provide the Ministry of Labour in April of each year. The data for 1978 are shown in Table 28 which covers the textile industry as well as all other industrial branches of Americana.[53] Even though the breakdown of enterprises according to size is not as disaggregated as in the previous tables, it suggests that the very high number of small enterprises indicated by the 1975/76 surveys continues. It also reveals how Americana's economy is dominated by the textile industry; with its almost 600 enterprises and 18,000 workers[54] it accounts for around 60 per cent of the town's industry.

It is rare to find such comprehensive data on small-scale producers as those on Americana's textile industry. Most notable is the existence of registers which indicate whether a firm is independent or subcontracted (see Tables 24, 25 and 26). Significantly, these are not from the government's statistical office (IBGE), whose registers are

TABLE 28 Industrial branches of Americana: number of firms and workers according to size of firm, April 1978

Industry	Firms (total)	Workers (total)	Size of firm according to number of workers							
			0 – 50		51 – 200		201 – 500		500+	
			Firms	Workers	Firms	Workers	Firms	Workers	Firms	Workers
Mineral extraction	5	29	5	29	-	-	-	-	-	-
Food	28	234	28	234	-	-	-	-	-	-
Drinks	1	2	1	2	-	-	-	-	-	-
Textiles	592	18,206	533	5818	45	4533	9	2724	5	5131
Shoes, clothing	33	660	30	481	3	179	-	-	-	-
Wood, cork	7	33	7	33	-	-	-	-	-	-
Furniture	17	173	16	122	1	51	-	-	-	-
Printing	7	101	7	101	-	-	-	-	-	-
Leather, skins	1	33	1	33	-	-	-	-	-	-
Rubber	3	1768	2	6	-	-	-	-	1	1762
Chemical, pharmaceutical	4	29	4	29	-	-	-	-	-	-
Plastics	4	49	4	49	-	-	-	-	-	-
Glass, cement, bricks/ceramics	19	171	19	171	-	-	-	-	-	-
Metallurgical	28	3341	22	270	1	139	4	1224	1	1708
Machinery, electrics/electronics	40	883	36	178	3	238	1	467	-	-
Vehicles	41	196	41	196	-	-	-	-	-	-
Building	178	2045	169	1150	9	835	-	-	-	-
Energy	1	70	-	-	1	70	-	-	-	-
Others	10	35	10	35	-	-	-	-	-	-
Total	1019	28,058	935	8937	63	6105	14	4415	7	8601

Source: Ministry of Labour, '2/3 Survey', April 1978.

comparatively deficient, as confirmed by the director of its local office. This is somewhat surprising, because, as mentioned before, it is rare to find an unregistered enterprise in Americana. This was confirmed by both the small and large producers interviewed, as well as by trade union officials and the director of the local labour office. The reasons for this are that control and inspection are relatively tough, that parent firms only farm out work to subcontractors who are registered, and workers themselves demand registration. All this is perhaps connected with the stage of industrial development reached in Americana and in the state of São Paulo, which, in Brazilian terms, is very advanced.

Short History of Subcontracting

The textile industry of Americana dates back to the early years of this century when a cotton spinning and weaving mill was established.[55] It took a further two decades for a second mill to be set up, in this case a mill which produced silk cloth.

At the beginning of the thirties, weavers of these factories began to invest their savings in second-hand looms which they upgraded and installed in their own homes. They obtained yarn from their employers to be woven into cloth by wives and daughters working at home, while initially they continued to work as internal employees. Gradually they left their employment and began working exclusively as subcontractors, either for their former employers or for yarn dealers from São Paulo (capital). These were intermediaries (commercial capital) who bought yarn, distributed it among small producers to have it woven into cloth and then collected and sold it in São Paulo.

It was during the forties that Americana's weavers took their great leap forward. The Second World War had brought a rapid rise in Brazilian textile exports, in the wake of which new markets opened up, bringing Americana's weavers more work.[56] In addition, one of Brazil's largest and most powerful yarn producers, Matarazzo, contributed to the multiplication of small

133

subcontracted weaving sheds by delivering considerable quantities of cellulosic yarn (rayon) to Americana. Most of this yarn passed through the hands of an industrialist whom we interviewed. He reported that he received the yarn on credit, distributed it amongst local small producers and had up to a thousand looms working for him in such subcontracted workshops.

The end of the Second World War and the subsequent regaining of world markets by the leading industrial nations brought an end to the period of rapid and easy growth, and crisis to Brazil's textile industry. How serious this crisis was in Americana is not clear from our sources of information.[57] What seems clear is that over the following three decades the town's textile industry expanded; independent and subcontracted producers increased in numbers and some also in size. A few managed the transition from subcontractor to independent producer in these years.[58] Apparently the process of growth was interrupted by various crises caused by the introduction of new taxes, shortages of raw material and problems of overproduction. These hit the subcontractors particularly hard. Unfortunately no written accounts or statistics are available on this period, but in what follows an attempt is made to bring out the main features of the subcontracting system and the problems encountered by the producers involved.

The Parent Firm's Interest

Many of the firms which are now of medium or large size owe their growth to the use of external subcontracted workshops. In the case of four of the six sample firms of medium and large size, the putting out system was a major means of accumulation. (The other two firms were of more recent origin and subsidaries of multinationals.) For many years all four firms had more looms working for them outside than inside their factories. In particular during their initial years of operation, their capital went to a large extent into the purchase of yarn which they distributed amongst small producers and then collected again in the form of cloth. This enabled them to expand production without investment in machinery or buildings.

Indeed, the parent firms emphasised that one of the main reasons for their use of subcontractors was <u>not to immobilise their capital</u>, or, in other words, to use their financial resources as circulating capital and not as fixed capital. Today the internal production of these firms is higher than the subcontracted part, for reasons to be explained later. However, the profits required to buy their own machinery were largely earned through the subcontracting system.

The second reason for using this system lies in the flexibility it offers the parent firms. Working with an external workforce enables them to adjust smoothly to irregularities in demand. In the words of the director of one of the firms, 'subcontracting is for us a resource to draw upon when demand is high, it enables us to increase our production quickly when we need to.' Of course the same applies the other way round; in periods of sluggish demand, it is easy for them to reduce production, or as another manager put it, 'the subcontractors provide a safety valve' to the parent firms. Four of the five medium and large firms which had, or used to have, subcontractors affirmed that this facility was one of the main reasons for working with them. For example, the biggest firm to make use of subcontractors had reduced its number of external looms from over 1000 in 1976 to 500 in 1978/79, mainly due to marketing problems.

Subcontracting can also help in coping more easily with 'awkward' orders. In fact, one of the multinationals, being geared to large-scale production, kept subcontractors mainly in order to cope with small orders. In relation to total production the subcontracting was of little importance to this firm, but it was important for its ability to respond flexibly to customer demand. (The other multi-national firm was not involved in subcontracting at all.)

A third reason for subcontracting is related to differences in labour costs between parent firms and subcontractors. All respondents affirmed that wages paid by the subcontractors were lower than those paid for comparable jobs in parent firms and in our comparisons they were found to be at last one-third lower. However, opinions in parent firms were divided on whether subcontracted production cost them less than internal production. The main issue here is that the cloth woven by the subcontractors tends to be of lower quality. A few subcontractors have moved up-market and specialised in high-quality items, but they are the exception. Since the parent firms pay by the metre, the subcontractors' main concern is generally to maximise output rather than achieve high and constant quality, which suffers further because, paying low wages, the subcontractors cannot keep their best workers. The manager of one parent firm stated that his internal production costs were lower than those for subcontracted production because of this problem of quality. The other firms also emphasised this problem and therefore farmed out only that part of their production in which quality mattered least. In these lines they found that subcontracting did give them a slightly lower cost per unit of output.

The Subcontractors

The people who become subcontractors usually come from the internal labour force of textile firms. Of the fourteen subcontractors interviewed, thirteen had previously been employees and had worked either as weavers or foremen. This pattern was confirmed by all other respondents.

Asked why they had left their wage employment, the subcontractors were unanimous: in order to improve their economic, and thus also social situation. Families relying on a weaver's wage can hardly escape poverty unless there are other sources of income. While foremen or supervisors earn a higher wage, employees' career prospects are not found sufficiently promising. Also they prefer to be their own masters. Thus, many try their luck and set up their own business. We will show later how and why quite a few of them fail, but this does not change the major point to be emphasised here, which is that the subcontractors are former employees who seek economic and social advance outside wage employment.

What is needed to set up one's own business? The parent firm delivers the yarn which the subcontractors transform into cloth. The yarn for the warp is generally provided ready wound on a beam; the yarn for the weft is delivered on cones, which the subcontractors wind on to pirns to fit the shuttles of their looms. The machinery required consists of a winding machine and a minimum of four looms, as this is the number which one person can operate. The maintenance of the machines is up to the subcontractors. None of the respondents received technical assistance from the parent firms.

Generally, second-hand machinery is used, bought in most cases from independent firms or other subcontractors who have modernised or gone out of business; in some cases it is bought from a dealer in second-hand machinery. The initial investment in machinery is as follows: four mechanical looms, at around Cr$ 10,000 each, comes to Cr$ 40,000, including all accessories. A mechanical winder costs approximately Cr$ 2000.[59] Thus, the initial capital required for machinery is Cr$ 42,000 which is equivalent to around eight months' wages of a weaver employed by an independent firm.

Buying his own machinery is therefore feasible and not entirely out of reach for a weaver. In fact, some begin with a greater number of looms and most buy additional looms once they have gained initial experience as subcontractors. What is generally beyond their means is to become independent producers; that is, buy the raw material, transform it into cloth and sell it. First, the working capital needed to buy raw material is well above the investment in machinery. Second, the quantity of yarn required would be too small to be of interest to yarn suppliers. Hence the workers begin as subcontractors, but hope that it will be possible to accumulate and one day produce independently.

As there is a constant flow of new entrants into the branch, competition amongst subcontractors is intense. The interviews showed clearly that they find themselves unable to negotiate the piece rates, having little choice but to accept the parent firms' terms. Differences in what parent firms offer are very slight. In the words of one small producer, 'it is easy for them to find subcontractors, there are always those willing to offer their services and accept their conditions.'

Payment is lowest for those who are secondary subcontractors, that is, those who do not receive the work directly from the parent firm, but from an intermediary, the primary subcontractors. Such intermediaries generally, though not always, have their own production facilities and do part of the job received from the parent firm themselves, while giving out to other producers that part of the weaving they cannot do. This two-tier system occurs mainly when the parent firm is not from Americana, but the capital city São Paulo. In total, approximately half the subcontracted production seems to be for parent firms from São Paulo and half for local parent firms.

In order to undermine the power of the parent firms there have been attempts to organise the subcontractors. The first dates back to 1941 when a cooperative[60] was formed, through which small producers gained access to raw material and began to produce and sell their cloth. However, the stronger members of the cooperative gained increasing control of the organisation and finally turned it into a private company in 1944.

Later organisational attempts were limited to bringing the subcontractors together into an association with the objective of establishing better piece rates with parent firms. Associations with this objective can only work if all the members adhere to the agreed policy. As some respondents recorded, there were always those who accepted work for lower rates than those fixed by the association, when they were faced with a substantial reduction in work, or with a complete standstill. Thus, when survival is at stake, the subcontractor generally makes all possible efforts to keep going in order to cover at least his fixed costs such as instalments on machinery, rent for workshop, or payment for accountancy. Such practices undermine collective action and indeed none of the attempted associations survived for long.

Usually the months from December to February are slack and subcontractors have to reduce the number of hours worked or the number of looms in operation. For those with workers from outside the family this period is particularly difficult. The yearly wage increases for textile workers in the state of São Paulo come into force in November and producers reported that they generally do not manage to pass on the increased costs to the parent firms until March when business tends to pick up again.

What does most harm to the subcontractors are crises in which the parent firms give out little or no work for extended periods. Thus, the parent firm's ability to adjust easily to changes in demand constitutes the subcontractor's greatest problem. 'If they tell you tomorrow that they haven't got any work for you, there's nothing you can do ... they have no obligation towards you except to pay the agreed rate for the quantity of cloth you make.'

The interviews produced many accounts of subcontractors who had to give up in such crises and to return to wage employment, or others who only just managed to survive. For example, '1975 and 76 were good years and I had two employees, but 1977/78 was terrible and I had to fire them, cloth didn't sell, there was little work, and for one month I stopped completely. I was about to take on a job as an employee, but then some work came up and I got going again.' According to a former subcontractor who is now supervisor in another firm: 'There were always bad periods: once it was eight months in a single year. I had to reduce working hours, and finally I sold the machines, I couldn't go on. I sold the machines to another guy who wanted to try, but he didn't get very far either.' Other subcontractors were keen on pointing out that not all parent firms were hit equally and simultaneously by sluggish demand and that through clever manœuvering and with some luck they, as subcontractors, were able to avoid major crises. But these respondents emphasised the instability faced generally by sub-contractors. Although this is a major characteristic of subcontractor operations, it cannot be documented through detailed turnover rates of enterprises. However, corroborating evidence did emerge from the research. Thus, of the sample of subcontractors selected from a 1976 register of enterprises, only 50 per cent were still in business in 1979. This could partly reflect the quality of the register in that some of those producers might have gone out of business before 1976, but it reinforces the general impression of instability among such enterprises.

Employment and Income

How does this combination of circumstances affect employment and income in the subcontracted sector? The tough competition and the consequent low piece rates make it indispensable for the small owner to participate directly in the process of production, unless he has an additional source of income. Indeed, in the initial period, the owner is generally the main worker, and is in may cases aided by other members of his family. Thus wives not only do the housework, but often help with the winding of the yarn and with other odd jobs or even replace the husband at the looms when he has to leave the workshop.

The more the subcontractor expands, the more time he is required to give to managerial tasks. Even so, the largest subcontractor interviewed (eighty looms) went to great length to explain how he had only been able to grow and overcome crises because, whenever necessary, he himself had worked with his employees on the looms.

The working day in the subcontracted enterprises is very long: in all cases investigated it went beyond the eight-hour working day, which is the norm in medium and large-scale enterprises. All subcontractors said they worked at least ten hours a day, some up to twelve or thirteen. Shiftwork is impracticable for most subcontracted workshops since they are based to a large extent on family labour. Only one of the small subcontractors worked on a shift system; he had eight looms which were operated in the first shift by his wife and son, and in the second shift by two employees, the owner himself doing the additional work necessary to keep both shifts going. The largest of the subcontractors also worked in two shifts with his total of thirty-six employees.

As for payment, the remuneration of family workers depends on whether they belong to the owner's household or not. When they do not, they earn what an employed non-family worker would receive. In the case of weavers, the monthly wage was between Cr$ 3000 and Cr$ 4000 based on a ten-hour working day. In comparison, the weaver employed by an independent firm earns between Cr$ 5000 and Cr$ 6000 monthly based on an eight-hour working day, so that a weaver can earn up to twice as much if he works for an independent enterprise. This has immediate implications for the type of workers the subcontractor can attract. Some of these workers would not be accepted by independent firms because of advanced age or some handicap, others are not prepared to subject themselves to the tight rules and discipline imposed by most independent firms. More important, however, are the very young workers on whom the subcontractors rely heavily. They train them, work with them and then generally lose them once they have learnt their job. The young workers naturally move on to the independent producers who pay better and offer more stability.

If the wage earners in the subcontracted firms are so poorly paid, what about the subcontractors themselves? Given the intense competition and the power of the parent firms, can they earn more than the weavers' wage of Cr$ 5000 to 6000 or the foreman's wage of Cr$ 8000 to 9000 (in independent firms)? Several subcontractors provided detailed information on their monthly incomings and outgoings, which showed great consistency; they are shown in Table 29, assuming the case of a workshop in which the owner works with two employees and has eight looms. The subcontractor receives on average Cr$ 3200 per loom per month (e.g. monthly production per loom of 700 metres multiplied by the piece rate of Cr$ 4.60 per metre). For the production of the eight looms he is paid Cr$ 25,600. His monthly outgoings are as shown in Table 29.

As can be seen from these figures, the subcontractor with eight looms and two employees earns around Cr$ 9000 which is 50 per cent more than the wage of an employed weaver and the same as the wage for a foreman. If, however, we consider all the benefits which the employee receives but which the subcontractor foregoes (e.g. paid holidays, thirteenth monthly wage, guarantee fund) and consider his longer working hours, he is only slightly better off than the employed weaver and falls behind the foreman. If the workshop were his own, the situation would be somewhat better, but most subcontractors work in

TABLE 29 Monthly outgoings of a small subcontractor

(in Cr$ of 1979)

Rent of workshop[a]	2100
Wear and tear of machines (spare parts, repairs)	700
Electricity	2000
Accountancy	1200
Wage for one weaver	3600
Wage for one auxiliary worker	2200
Social security payments, thirteenth monthly wage and other costs incurred for two employees above	2900
Threader	600
Owner's health insurance and pension fund[b]	1300
Total	16,600

Notes:

a. This does not include living quarters.

b. While this constitutes a benefit to the owner, it should be included under costs to make the subcontractor's income comparable with an employee's wage.

rented workshops. Also, if his wife and children can do the auxiliary work, the comparison may show the subcontractor as being better off.

The income of a producer with only four looms (owner with one other worker) would lag behind the employed weaver's wage, unless the subcontractor has his own workshop and is helped by a family member. The majority of subcontractors have between eight and twenty-four looms. Twenty-four, for instance, imply a total labour force of nine workers.

Obviously each step of expansion provides the possibility of higher income, but also increases risks. The major risk is that of periods of insufficient work for the machinery installed, which alternate with periods of working to full capacity. The subcontractor's income follows the ups and downs in the textile industry very closely. As one of them put it, 'there are good months when I earn a lot more than I could possibly earn as an employee and there are bad months when I would be better off if I was employed.'

The Future of Subcontracting

None of the respondents saw the future of small subcontractors in rosy terms. Nevertheless, they said that workers continue to try to set up their own business, and indeed two of the producers interviewed were newcomers. Of those who had been in operation for longer, most wanted to continue as, on balance, they found they were doing better than they could have done as employees, but emphasised that this was as a result of hard work. What kept them going was also the ever present hope of a couple of good years and making it in the end.

The disillusioned were carrying on, even though they did not fare better than employees, for a variety of reasons: they preferred to be their own boss and wanted to organise their own timetable (even if it meant working, in total, longer hours), some also feared that because of their advanced age securing a good job as an employee (e.g. foreman) could be problematic; a machinery supplier also mentioned that considerations of pride and status kept subcontractors from returning to wage employment. Of those interviewees who had given up, none was prepared to try it again, mainly because of fear of the instability of work and income, 'working as a subcontractor gives more headache than money'.

As for the medium and long-term tendencies of the subcontracting system, the majority of the respondents - parent firms, subcontractors and machinery suppliers - believed that it was in decline. All parent firms had cut back on their subcontracted production. Part of this was a short-term phenomenon, because in January 1979 most of them were undergoing a relatively slack period. But all these firms also showed a clear long-run trend to move away from subcontracting and towards producing inside their own factories.

One of the reasons relates to a point made earlier; parent firms repeatedly claimed that subcontractors could not meet the quality standards of their own internal production.[61] The explanation for the low quality can easily be deduced from what was said before: low pay forces the subcontractor to (a) pay low wages and (b) outdo the parent firm whenever possible, both of which result in lower product quality. In turn, parent firms tend to farm out only those lines in which quality matters least and these are more often than not the lines in which competition is toughest and profits are lowest and in which they are least inclined to increase their payment of subcontractors. There are exceptions to this tendency, but the general situation is as described.

There is, however, a much more compelling reason for the decline in subcontracting, which has begun to make itself felt and which will develop its full force in the years to come, namely the technological development in weaving. The majority of subcontractors use mechanical looms and one weaver can operate four or five of these at a time. The looms are bound to be replaced gradually by automatic looms, as the latter bring about at least a doubling in labour productivity; one weaver can operate ten automatic looms and their speed is greater.

This affects the subcontracting system first and foremost because the initial investment in machinery rises considerably. A new automatic loom costs between Cr$ 160,000 and Cr$ 200,000. Furthermore, if the producer decides to modernise he cannot change gradually from mechanical to automatic looms as he expands. Since one weaver can operate ten automatic looms at a time, he has to buy a minimum of ten machines. This means an investment of around Cr$ 2,000,000. If the producer can find ten looms second-hand and in good condition, he might be able to get them for Cr$ 800,000. In addition he needs at least two automatic winders which each cost Cr$ 60,000 new or around Cr\$ 25,000 second-hand. So, taking second-hand machinery prices, the initial investment would be Cr\$ 850,000. This has to be compared with Cr\$ 84,000 which is necessary to start up with, for example, eight mechanical looms and two mechanical winders. Hence the entry barrier into the branch is increased enormously.

To conclude, in most types of weaving, the mechanical looms cannot compete with automatic looms. The investment necessary for the more modern looms is beyond the means of many subcontractors, considering that most of them are former employees who buy the machinery in instalments and with savings made from their wages. Given that the initial investment in automatic machinery corresponds to around 160 months' wages, the number of subcontractors is likely to decrease.

According to our respondents, some products will continue to be woven on the mechanical loom, in particular acetate and very fine or second-rate rayon and nylon. These yarns are not strong enough to be woven on automatic looms; they could be woven on these machines, but the frequent stoppages do not make it worthwhile. Machinery suppliers emphasised that future development would remedy this, but confirmed that for the time being the mechanical loom would continue to be used for these yarns. In these lines, the subcontractors are therefore less threatened by technological change.[62]

Another factor working against the small subcontractors is the increasing difficulty in finding inexpensive premises. The visitor to Americana can hardly miss the presence of the weaving industry; the rhythmic noise of the looms accompanies one throughout most of the districts of the town, be they residential or industrial. The local government, in line with a programme of the state government, is now trying to reduce the noise pollution and move the weaving sheds out of the town centre and the residential areas and place them in special industrial districts.

Those firms which are located in the residential areas are allowed to continue, but no firm is allowed to set up a new factory or workshop. If a firm sells its premises with all the machinery installed the buyer is allowed to take over and continue producing in this location. If the seller dismantles the machinery and removes it from the building, it cannot be used for industrial purposes. This policy hits the subcontractors in quite a devastating way. Those who want to open up a new weaving shed have only two options: the first is to find somebody who is giving up and take over his entire business; this means buying his machinery and buying or renting the building, but only in fortuitous circumstances would they find a workshop of the desired size and type at the time they needed it. The other option would be to move into the new industrial districts, which implies buying a plot and building a new weaving shed, an investment which is far beyond the means of small subcontractors. The conjuncture of these restrictions and the technological development is bound to bring about a decline in the subcontracting system. Such a decline is not likely to occur as a sudden exodus of subcontractors, but rather as those who give up because of a temporary crisis or retirement are not replaced, as in the past.

In this sense, we believe that a decrease in the number of subcontractors is almost certain to occur. It seems even clearer that subcontracted production as a percentage of total production is going to decrease; all investigated parent firms had been increasing their internal production and cut back or at best kept constant their external production. Whether the total output produced by subcontractors will be reduced in absolute terms is difficult to say. First, there are those fibres for which the old machinery is still advantageous and where subcontracting can continue in small-scale operations. Second, it is conceivable that some subcontractors who specialise in the production of small quantities of high-quality products can survive. Third, and most importantly, a few subcontractors seem to be able to change to automatic looms; one of the subcontractors interviewed had bought such machines second-hand and according to the machinery suppliers this was not an isolated case. Hence a smaller number of subcontractors might well produce the same or even greater output, but in relation to the internal production of independent firms there can be little question that it is declining.

A New Pattern of Labour Utilisation

If our analysis is correct, then an era of Americana's textile industry is gradually coming to an end. Until recently two of its main features were, first, the transition from wage employment to subcontractor which was attempted by many workers, even though only a few could finally manage to set up as independent producers. Second, those independent enterprises which managed to grow into large firms did so largely through the extensive use of subcontractors. These features of Americana's industry are slowly but clearly declining in importance. The recent arrival of mulitinationals has not in itself provoked major changes in this growth pattern. It merely reinforced the tendencies described, since these firms are technologically very advanced and use subcontracting very little, if at all.

To assess their impact on the home-grown medium and large firms, one should distinguish between competition in the product market and changes brought about in the labour market. In product markets, the international firms are not in direct competition with the local firms,[63] in fact, the interviews confirm the picture already mentioned of a very segmented textile market. In the labour market, the international firms caused some temporary shortages at the time of initiating production, but the overall effect has been to increase the labour supply in Americana. The town has gained a reputation for having a particularly booming industry and offering good job opportunities; this is directly related to the establishment of subsidiaries of several multinational firms, not only in textiles but also in other industries. This undoubtedly contributed to migration to Americana and a surplus of labour in the area, the clearest indication of which were queues of job seekers in front of factory gates.

In terms of labour demand, the multinationals seem to be at the forefront of establishing a new pattern of labour utilisation in the textile industry, in particular with regard to recruitment and training. They were found to prefer production workers without previous experience in the industry. This was particularly puzzling as there was not just a surplus of labour, but that surplus included people

147

who had previously worked in textiles. A similar recruitment policy was found in some mills in the North East, briefly referred to in the previous case study. What seems to account for this policy is not so much foreign ownership in itself as the new technology. Interviews with workers, managers, machinery suppliers and textile consultants, carried out in Americana and in other textile centres previously, revealed that the skill requirements for machine operators had diminished with technological modernisation. From conversations with managers in particular we conclude that higher training costs incurred by recruiting young unskilled workers are outweighed by gains in discipline and control over labour in the workplace. Thus, in terms of changes in the overall employment pattern in the industry, there is on the one hand the relative decline in external or indirect labour use (subcontracting) and on the other a relative increase in internal or direct labour use, accompanied by a process of de-skilling. In other terminology this represents a shift from formal to real subordination of labour (Marx, 1969).

This issue of the impact of technological change on the utilisation of labour is very complex (see e.g. Bell, 1972; Braverman, 1974; Davis, 1972; Schmitz, 1980) and has only been mentioned briefly. One reason for raising it here lies in the changes which this brings about in the transfer of skills between small and large enterprises. Until recently there was a clearly established flow of skills in both directions. As already observed, most subcontractors had been weavers or foremen employed in independent firms, which amounts to a transference of skills from the independent to subcontracted enterprises. In reverse, young workers trained by the subcontractors used to move on to independent enterprises; in fact, both subcontractors and spokesmen for the parent firms confirmed that over the last four decades the subcontractors have trained a large part of the workforce of independent firms. This is changing now with the new technology which tends both to reduce the emergence of small subcontractors and induce large firms to recruit young unskilled workers.

Notes

1   This applies mainly to the clothing and hammock industry and less to the weaving industry.

2   The number and type of respondents are given separately in each study.

3   See Appendix.

4   More recently (1979 and 1980) the debate in the national and international press has concentrated on how the Brazilian economy can cope with a huge and increasing foreign debt and with the easing of political repression and the rising militancy of the labour unions.

5   For a detailed study of the minium wage see Calsing (1978).

6   It is also a vigorously discussed issue; see Macedo and Garcia (1978) and Souza and Baltar (1979).

7   This is not to say that denationalisation only started after 1964.

8   While Evans' and Newfarmer's work illustrates very clearly the constraints which national firms can be up against in branches where foreign capital is heavily involved, it is not discussed in detail because the enterprises studied are large compared to those which are the focus of this work.

9   The following brief account draws on Versiani (1971), Evans (1979) and IPEA (1976).

10 The most recent census available is of 1970. An industrial census was carried out in 1975, but at the time of writing the results had not been published.

11 As in a recent study of the clothing industry (BNB, BNDE, SUDENE, 1977, Vol.II) which was commissioned by the government and carried out by a private consultancy firm which enjoys a good reputation for expertise on clothing manufacture.

12 A detailed study of outworkers in the clothing industry of Rio de Janeiro is being carried out by Alice de Paiva Abreu, Instituto Universitário de Pesquisas do Rio de Janeiro.

13 This is based on conversations with persons who have a good knowledge of the local industry in São Paulo (city), Rio de Janeiro (city), Juiz de Fora and Fortaleza. The case

study carried out in Petrópolis provides further support.

14   Summarised at the beginning of the case study on the hammock industry.

15   For instance, Goodman and Cavalcanti (1974), while very critical of SUDENE practices in general, accept the validity of its survey results and make no reference to the corresponding census data. On the other hand, Sandmeyer (1976) bases his study on the Industrial Census figures only.

16   The most comprehensive interpretation of the Brazilian Industrial Census data relating to small (and medium) enterprises is provided by Gonçalves (1976), covering the period 1950-70; the validity of the census data is however taken for granted in his study.

17   The interviews for this case study were carried out in conjunction with Líscio Camargo in July/August 1977.

18   Broadly speaking, the interviews with producers covered two areas: the internal functioning of the firm and the relationships with other firms. As the focus of this work is on small-scale industry, only that information from the large and medium-sized enterprises which has a bearing on this question was used here.

19   The sources consulted were: the Industrial Census of IBGE; the register of firms of the '2/3 survey' of the Ministry of Labour; the Ministry of Finance's register of firms used for the purpose of taxation of industrial products (IPI), and the register of firms of the municipality of Petrópolis, used for taxation of services (ISS).

20   The problems are manifold: knitting and clothing firms are in some cases classified with spinning and weaving firms, in other cases with shoe firms, and data on numbers of workers are incomplete or entirely lacking.

21   In the state of Rio de Janeiro one minimum wage was, in July 1977, Cr$ 1106.40 = US$ 74.00 (US$ 1 = Cr$ 15 in second half of 1977).

22   For an assessment of the debate on appropriate technology and problems of definition see Stewart (1978).

23   The higher yarn costs for the small producers cannot be explained by the fact that they often receive supplier credit, because the larger producers can count on even longer periods for payment.

24   One problem here would be the high investment in

circular knitting machines which the large producers use for their lighter articles; but the small producers could buy the knitted cloth from the larger ones and make it up into garments, as in fact some already do.

25   These estimates are annexed to this case study.

26   It is likely that the Population Census classified the weavers who work in the hammock industry with the weavers of the weaving industry and not as hammock makers.

27   In the case of the registered enterprises, a random selection was made from the 1976 register of enterprises of the '2/3 survey' of the Ministry of Labour, supplied by the Human Resources Department of SUDENE. The inclusion of non-registered enterprises was governed by the possibilities of access gained through various informal contacts.

28   While somewhat folkloric, this is the most comprehensive source on the history of production and use of hammocks. Otherwise the most useful study found was by Rios e Associados (1962). It is also worth mentioning a survey carried out by the Núcleo de Assistência Industrial (1975) on the textile industry of the state of Paraíba which takes in hammock-making, including some aspects of production, machinery and labour force. After the drafting of our study, two further research reports on the hammock industry in the state of Paraíba were received: Polonordeste (1979) and Rocha (1979).

29   According to an interview with one of the pioneers of industrial hammock production in Fortaleza.

30   Prices refer to July 1978, when the official exchange rate was US$ 1 = Cr$ 18.

31   A small wastage of yarn is permitted.

32   Since this is a case of 'disguised wage labour' it is analysed in greater detail in a section on external labour.

33   There are even signs that the ability of many hammock producers to obtain yarn in the desired quantity depends on being given a quota by this particular supplier.

34   The average production of a manually operated loom can be put at ten hammocks a day.

35   In a large and small firm labour productivity can be considered equal, at least to the extent that it depends on

technological conditions.

36 No data are available on the costs of electricity, wear and tear on equipment, office, transport of hammocks, etc. However, this should not affect to any great extent a comparison between small and large enterprises, and in any case, it was not calculated in the costs of the small enterprise.

37 One point which is not fully understood is why some producers do not transfer their enterprise to the North (Amazonas or Pará), which is one of the main markets, has no hammock production, but has (as the North East) abundant labour. The reason possibly lies in the long tradition of hammock production in Ceará and the ease with which experienced workers can be found (economies of agglomeration). On the other hand, the work is not highly skilled and training workers is not too difficult.

38 Except where dyeing of the yarn is a factor.

39 A standard hammock takes three hours to produce, while the luxury version can take more than two days, chiefly because of the different type of finishing.

40 The FGTS (Fundo de Garantia do Tempo de Serviço) is built up by employer's monthly payments equal to 8 per cent of the remuneration paid to the employee in the previous month.

41 As of May 1978-April 1979.

42 There is one group of local (Fortaleza) importance which makes hammocks, but they are not its main product.

43 Further empirical work on technology and employment in the spinning and weaving industry is being carried out (Schmitz, 1980). For a theoretical approach see Brighton Labour Process Group (1977).

44 The starting point was the 1976 Register of Enterprises, used for Table 16: some firms had since closed down, others had entered the branch, giving a total of thirty-three firms.

45 This would be equivalent, for example, to seventy-four producers each with an average of four looms.

46 Also the Ceará Survey of Enterprises, carried out in 1972 by the Superintêndencia do Desenvolvimento do Estado do Ceará (SUDEC), does not fill this gap. See SUDEC (1973a) and BANDECE (1973, Appendix).

47 See Table 16.

48 Provided by the textile employers' federation of the state of São Paulo.

49 These percentages could be somewhat exaggerated, because statistical coverage for the state of São Paulo tends to be more complete than for most other states.

50 Comparable information is not available for other states but our impression is that subcontracting in the state of São Paulo is more common than in other states of Brazil.

51 The table is based on a register of enterprises which was prepared by the Textile Workers' Union of Americana and kindly provided for this research.

52 This can probably be explained as follows: first, no enterprises without employees are included, as the register is based on information on fees which each firm has to transfer to the union annually for each worker; second, not all small producers with employees are included; this is concluded from the fact that several such producers were interviewed, but could not be found in this register. In relation to larger enterprises, however, the data seem to be accurate.

53 This table was kindly provided by the director of the local labour office. It had been prepared by another researcher for a different project and is simply reproduced here. It was not possible to check it against the register of enterprises and employees on which it is based and thus compare it firm by firm with the register prepared by the textile workers' union.

54 The number of 18,206 textile workers in Table 28 looks surprisingly high, especially in relation to the union survey (Table 27) which indicated a total of only 14,701 workers. Even though the latter suffers from various omissions explained above, and the two surveys do not refer to the same months of 1978, these factors are unlikely to account for the total difference.

55 This historical section is based upon interviews with two retired industrialists and on FIDAM (1971).

56 Brief references to this period in the literature give the impression that Americana's cloth was exported, whereas our respondents claimed that the increased

production was sold internally in a generally expanding market.

Similarly, as regards the expansion of the textile industry during that period, one study on small and medium-sized firms (Vieira, 1968) states that the Second World War did not facilitate the setting up of textile enterprises in the interior of the state of São Paulo; this does not correspond to information received in the interviews.

57 Given the uncertainty of information it is difficult to establish a clear link between the changes in Brazil's relationships with the central economies during the thirties and forties and the growth of Americana's textile industry. The secondary literature, in particular Versiani (1971), provides data on the changes in Brazilian production and exports during the forties; these statistics refer, however, to cotton cloth, whereas the main yarn woven by Americana's subcontractors during that time was rayon.

58 Several firms were reported to have begun as subcontractors in those years, even though only one of the independent firms of the sample started as a subcontractor at that time.

59 These are average prices for second-hand machinery as of early 1979. The official exchange rate at the beginning of 1979 was US$ 1 = Cr$ 22.

60 Cooperativa Industrial de Tecidos Rayon de Americana (CITRA).

61 One should, of course, expect a tendency among parent firms to stress this quality problem as a way of 'justifying' the low piece rates. But the fact that they have cut back on subcontracting over the years would tend to confirm that their 'complaints' are not entirely without foundation.

62 Natural silk is also still woven on mechanical looms but the raw material is so expensive, and high quality weaving so important that silk manufacturers prefer to weave inside their factories rather than subcontract others.

63 This does not exclude the possibility that home-grown industries elsewhere were directly affected, a question we cannot judge on the basis of our information.

PART 3

LESSONS FROM THE CASE STUDIES

Caution is necessary in making generalisations from such a small number of case studies. However, it is believed that these detailed studies of a limited number of activities have provided some insights which escape most large-scale surveys aiming at statistically generalisable findings. In a methodological section at the end of this final part, the advantages and limitations of both approaches will be discussed. Prior to this, we shall try to establish the general implications which can be drawn from the three case studies and discuss in which aspects they can or cannot advance our understanding of the issues brought out in the literature reviewed in Part 1. To this end, we shall examine the employment and income pattern which emerged in the three branches (referring to the issues raised in section 1.2) and then attempt to assess the question of the growth potential and constraints (referring to the issues raised in section 1.1).

3.1 <u>Employment, Income and Mobility</u>

The case studies reveal very clearly that characterising employment in the small-scale sector in terms of workers unable to find a job in a large enterprise or 'in terms of the source of employment of the urban poor' (Sethuraman, 1976, p.75) would be very misleading. They underline the necessity to differentiate when investigating earning opportunities in the small-scale sector: the main distinction should be between <u>owners of enterprises and their wage workers,</u> even though the former are themselves sometimes disguised wage workers of large enterprises. In this section we shall review the various types of employment situations found and discuss what they imply in terms of income and mobility.

Probably the single clearest finding which emerges in all three case studies is that the small-scale producers (owners) are not unsuccessful job seekers, but rather the contrary: they tend to be skilled workers who have left their jobs of their own accord. This is most obvious in the case of Americana's weavers and the clothing producers of Petrópolis. It is also true, though to a less extent, in the hammock industry of Fortaleza. The respondents find that setting up their own business gives a better chance for economic and social advance than wage employment.[1] Obviously this route for upward mobility is not open to all workers; only some can or want to try it. Nevertheless, it is a significant factor in explaining the emergence of new enterprises. It also means that small-scale production cannot be seen as a direct result of surplus labour taking refuge in these activities;[2] the labour surplus only has an indirect bearing in that its existence contributes to low wages, which in turn increase the desire to leave wage employment and to establish a business of one's own.

Indeed the main reason given for leaving a job is the low level of wages. The other reasons are all connected with an aspiration for 'independence'. This has a number of components which were mentioned in the course of the three case studies: employment in a factory usually means monotonous, repetitive work and following tight rules of discipline and timekeeping set by others. The possibilities of moving away from low wages and rigid work conditions through promotion are limited and in any case decided upon by others. By setting up his own business the worker hopes to take all this into his own hands. Being one's own master certainly gives more flexibility to organise work around other tasks or to absent oneself from work should the need arise. This freedom is highly valued, even though those who enjoy it often work longer hours than the wage workers.

The aspiration to 'independence' is in many ways an illusion. By escaping factory work, many do not entirely escape wage work; unable to buy their own raw material they have to turn to larger firms and perform piece work for these firms in their own small workshops. Thus, in relation to the larger firms, they are disguised wage labour or, if they employ workers themselves, they are the masters of a disguised wage labour force; hence they are not so much capitalists as agents of capital. This was most common among the subcontracted weavers of Americana; it was also frequent among the hammock producers of

Fortaleza, whereas the case of the clothing producers of Petrópolis is more complicated: they buy their own raw material and yet often end up in a type of piece work arrangement with other firms on whom they depend to market their product.

Scott (1979), who made similar observations in Peru, suggests that

> at the level of consciousness ... discrepancies emerge between the real and perceived situations of economic independece. This is partly a result of the form of remuneration, which by taking the form of "payment by results" gives the worker a feeling of freedom to decide when, where and how hard he will work; partly it is a reflection of the fact that his subjection to capital is only partial, and that he still owns some of his means of production and thus has a material basis for a bourgeois consciousness. (p.121)

While we did not concentrate on questions of class consciousness, we found instances of the conflict, when the small producers complained on the one hand about the cost or unreliability of their wage workers and on the other about the conditions imposed on them by their employers (parent firms). They certainly showed great awareness of their own subordinated position, but saw the subcontracting as a stage they had to go through in order to be able eventually to buy their own raw materials and market their own products.

In all three case studies it became apparent that many fail on their way up and eventually have to return to wage employment. Even though we are not in a position to quantify the failure rate, there can be no question that this attempt to achieve upward mobility is a very risky one. Nevertheless, it seems to be a risk worth taking, given that even the small producer who does not achieve 'full independence' and remains a subcontractor tends to earn more than he could as a wage worker. Recessions could destroy this advantage,[3] but the riskiness and instability of the small producers' work and income must be seen against high turnover rates among Brazilian factory workers which suggest that wage employment is far from stable.[4]

That the wage workers in Brazil are not privileged in any meaningful sense has been mentioned before and amply documented in studies which show the inadequacy of the wage for the reproduction of the worker and his family (DIEESE, 1973, 1974, 1975; Calsing, 1978). How the small-scale producers fare in relation to comparable wage workers has been little studied. The evidence collected in our case studies suggests that the small producers (owners) do better and are not an amalgamation of the poorest (in relative terms). The owner and his family sometimes earn through their joint labour more than if each went into wage employment, and even when they do not this comparison may not be sensible, because some members of the family cannot go out to work, women are often housebound looking after their children, adolescents have to study. In such circumstances the domestic enterprise is the most profitable if not the only way of increasing their income (a theme to which we will return later); hence the comparison to be made here is between the family's joint income and the wage which the head of household could earn in a large enterprise. It is not rare for the small firm owner to accept a lower real wage (per hour), in exchange for a (risky) opportunity to earn a greater amount by working longer hours and incorporating the labour of his family.

Let us now turn to the non-family wage workers employed in the small enterprises and compare their situation with that of wage workers in larger enterprises. In Fortaleza's hammock industry, the difference lay not in the money wage but in the benefits which the workers in small unregistered enterprises forego, especially health insurance. This also applied to the sewing women of Petrópolis. By contrast, in Americana, wage workers in small enterprises earned at least a third less than those in large enterprises, and in this case the job in the small enterprise was often the springboard for a better paid job in a large weaving firm. However, as was noted before, it is likely that this movement will gradually phase out with the direct recruitment of young unskilled workers by large firms.

The lowest level of remuneration for all categories of labour considered was that found among outworkers in the hammock industry. While they work with their own equipment and have a certain autonomy over the production process, they should not be conceived of as self-employed but as (disguised) wage workers used by both small and large enterprises. Since they are frequently housebound due to family obligations, bad health or old age, they tend to be stuck in the very bottom layer of the job market.

To sum up, in assessing the earning opportunities in the small-scale sector, two general conclusions arise from the case studies. First, distinctions must be made not only between owners of enterprises and wage workers, but also between types of owners (independent or subcontracted) and between types of workers (internal and outworkers). Second, setting up as a small-scale producer is often a route of upward mobility for wage workers rather than a mere survival strategy for unsuccessful job seekers. The first point has come to be increasingly emphasised in recent research. The second has not yet been given the importance it requires. Let us elaborate on both.

Several studies reviewed in Part 1 have brought out the need to differentiate between the earnings of owners and of wage workers in the small-scale sector. Moser (1978), Scott (1979) and Bromley and Gerry (1979) stress further the need to conceive of a continuum of employment situations stretching from the wage worker to the independent producer and draw attention in particular to intermediate categories, most notably that of disguised wage labour. The latter category was also used in this study, for the small subcontractor and for the outworker. Both have several features in common: they generally own the means of production (at least the implements of labour though not necessarily the raw materials), they have control to some extent over the production process, but cannot appropriate the surplus and are instead paid piece rates by the firm they work for. However, as was shown above, in terms of earnings they fare very differently. How can we explain this?

It is believed that the answer is linked to the distinction between small-scale production as a means of mobility and as a survival strategy.[5] Of course the two are not always easy to separate. As was reported in the case studies, workers starting new enterprises in order to improve on their wages often face so many difficulties that they have to fight for sheer survival. However, even if their enterprises fail, they generally have an <u>alternative</u> which is the return to wage employment. Outworkers do not usually have this alternative. Women are made housebound by the duties of child rearing and domestic work, or there are problems of age (children, old people) or poor health which leave no way out. In the latter case the lack of alternative is generally absolute, in the former there may be alternatives; but as pointed out in the recent literature which concentrates on women and the working poor, there are powerful cultural and ideological pressures which force women to stay at home and engage in those types of earning opportunities which are compatible with the domestic roles ascribed to them by society (Heyzer and Young, 1980; Moser, 1980). These pressures and the abundance of female labour keep the pay for outwork low; and the more this income is needed for survival the greater is the pressure to accept the conditions of the parent firms.

Stating that the small subcontractor, or for that matter the independent producer, has an alternative, does not imply that the alternavtive is an easy one. As pointed out before, combining business with domestic tasks is also of concern in those small enterprises; if the head of the enterprise returns to wage employment, it is often difficult to engage the family labour in gainful employment. Also, finding a satisfactory job might not always be easy for the head of the enterprise, considering the reported preference of some large enterprises for young unskilled workers. Nevertheless, the fact that most small producers have previous experience in wage work plus the wide variety of skills they possess, generally gives them a good chance of selling this skill and experience in the labour market. The availability of such alternatives is believed to be an important factor in the determination of earnings in the small-scale sector, and in distinguishing between those who work in it for survival and those to whom it offers possibilities for upward mobility.

Even though it is increasingly recognised in the literature that many small-scale producers earn more than wage workers of large enterprises, the prevailing perception is that small-scale activities are primarily but a means of survival. The experience from the case studies and Peattie's similar observations in the Colombian shoe industry (quoted in Part 1) lead us to suggest that at least in small-scale manufacturing the mobility hypothesis is more likely than the survival hypothesis. There would seem to be two critical questions which need to be considered in this investigation; one is the question of alternatives which has just been raised, the other is that of entry barriers to which we will turn now.

As pointed out in Part 1, the literature often describes the activities in which small-scale producers are prominent as being characterised by 'easy entry'. It would seem that this question needs more careful consideration, in particular clear distinctions must be made concerning what the 'ease' refers to. Clearly entry into the clothing, hammock or even weaving branch is easy in comparison to those branches of manufacturing where divisibility is restricted and where scale economies are important; an extreme example from the textile sector would be the continuous flow production of synthetic fibres. A different issue is that of entry barriers in relation to the newcomers to the urban labour market. The fact that small enterprises are in most cases set up by skilled workers suggests that entry into these branches is far from unrestricted. Previous knowledge of the branch seems to be a prerequisite; the minimum requirement is the ability to operate the machines, given that a good part of the work is generally carried out by the owner himself. The unskilled job seeker is unlikely to succeed as a small producer; his chances of finding a job in a large plant must be rated higher despite the limited absorptive capacity of such enterprises. In effect, there seems to be little reason why this particular aspect should be different in other branches of manufacturing. Given the small scale of operation, the new

161

producer has to master the entire production process. This requires a much wider variety of skills than work in large enterprises; the latter generally consists of a limited range of repetitive tasks which can be learned in a short time.

The other entry requirement is the capital necessary to buy the machinery. In the hammock industry this amounted to approximately US$ 1100 (for new equipment). In the weaving industry it came to approximately US$ 1900 (for second-hand equipment). In the knitting and clothing industry a complete set of new machinery would cost US$ 3600, but, as pointed out, the small producers in this industry rarely begin fully equipped, and, apart from the knitting machine itself, make do with cheaper temporary solutions; thus the initial capital requirement is nearer that of the other two branches. To give these capital requirements more meaning, they can be translated into the equivalent number of monthly wages of a skilled worker in the respective branch and town. In these terms, the initial investment is in the order of between eight and fourteen months' wages. Of course, this does not mean that those who are beginning have already saved the entire amount; in many cases they pay in instalments or borrow money through personal contacts. Nevertheless this constitutes a formidable entry barrier for those who start from scratch. It should, however, be added that identifying entry barriers in this sense does not necessarily mean lack of competition among those who have managed to overcome them. In fact, competition was found to be intense in all three case studies.

These findings will come as no surprise to those who have a first-hand knowledge of petty manufacturing, but they need emphasising in view of suggestions that 'a disproportionately large fraction of migrants, with very little own capital, schooling and experience, enter the informal sector' (Sethuraman, 1976, p.79). The situation is likely to be somewhat different in services and trade. Moser (1977), for instance, found that in Bogotá, 'despite individual cases of upward mobility ... small-scale marketing is a "refuge occupation" with a fair degree of recruitment in and little movement out (by death) as it increasingly absorbs from sectors such as agriculture and domestic service the unproductive labour surplus, the unskilled, old and women' (p.485). However, her study, as well as others (e.g. Bienefeld, 1974; Marga Institute, 1978), emphasise that even tertiary activities do not always constitute a free-for-all territory.

The link between entry barriers and mobility is not in all cases an easy one. Entry can be so difficult, due to high capital requirements or regulations imposed by producer associations or public bodies, that the possibility of setting up a new enterprise becomes very remote for any worker. Also, small producers can obtain their position through inheritance rather than through experience and savings from previous wage employment. Certainly further evidence is required from surveys based on work histories, which concentrate on the mode of skill and capital acquisition of small producers,[6] and which also link their different work situations with changes in their life cycle.[7] However, the identification of entry barriers is a first step towards establishing the likelihood of a branch becoming a refuge in which people with few resources crowd for their subsistence or an area into which only those who have previously accumulated certain skills, know-how and resources can graduate.

The mobility pattern outlined above provokes some additional thoughts on the question of class formation, which are not central to this work but should nevertheless be mentioned. The case studies suggest that the process of proletarianisation is far from linear and frequently interrupted: workers who used to earn their living by selling their labour power try to gain access to the means of production in the hope that by selling the product of their labour they can not only earn the equivalent of the invested labour time but also appropriate the surplus. In the branches where this occurs, it is probably not insignificant for the development of class consciousness and effective unionisation. Setting up one's own business for economic betterment can be an alternative to struggling in the factory for better wages and working conditions. Those who abandon factory work tend to be relatively skilled and courageous workers with a thorough understanding of the industry, but frustrated in their job.

The loss of these workers might be harmful to workers' attempts at effective organisation. Making a go of it on your own can become the accepted way to progress rather than joint action and solidarity.[8]

This was particularly apparent in Americana whose large textile workers' union has no real influence on wages and working conditions. Of course, after many years of state repression, weak trade unions are the rule rather than the exception in Brazil (or at least were until 1979). But Americana is particularly dominated by one industry, more than half of the industrial workforce belongs to the textile workers' union, yet there are no signs of it ever having been effective in its history. One must presume that this weakness was partly due to the widespread aspiration of workers in this town to set up their own business, even though this aspiration could only be realised by relatively few.

3.2 Determinants of Accumulation

The objective of this section is to return to the debate on internal and external growth constraints reviewed in Part 1 and assess what bearing the case studies have on the propositions put forward in the literature.

Internal Factors

Let us begin with those propositions which see lack of entrepreneurship and skills as obstacles to the growth of small enterprises. While these personal attributes relating to the owners of small enterprises are difficult to assess empirically, it is believed that the distinction made earlier is helpful here, namely that between questions of (a) drive, commitment, inventiveness, (b) technical skills,[9] and (c) organisational skills.

Even though the attributes under (a) are the most elusive, in-depth interviews can provide good impressions about these aspects of entrepreneurship. It is hoped that the three case studies convey some sense of the dedication, initiative, hard work, readiness to jump at opportunities, preparedness to take risks which we found among many of the respondents.[10] Surviving in a situation of illegality and tough competition requires a combination of hard work and alertness. Starting a business and trying to accumulate under conditions of great instability (as described) is not for those averse to taking risks. Also their commitment is beyond doubt: setting up as a small producer is clearly not a temporary vehicle which is abandoned once the possibility of a job as an employee arises. On the contrary, employees become small entrepreneurs in the hope of eventually expanding their businesses.

As regards technical skills, they have already been discussed in relation to entry barriers. In this context it suffices to say that they rarely constitute a problem, in fact thorough knowledge of the production process tends to be the small producer's strong point. The most important source of skill and know-how found was previous wage employment. Of course the training and experience gained in this way varied with the job occupied;[11] but generally it provided a sufficient basis to pick up the missing technical aspects through a process of learning-by-doing, which is an integral part of the small producer's struggle for survival or expansion.

Finally, the question of organisational skills has to be evaluated in the context of (a) the small firm's need for improvisation and flexibility and (b) the family set up. Both emerged as central features in the case studies, and, as pointed out before, set severe limits to advance planning and organisation, such that the outside observer might easily get the impression of organisational chaos. They are also both linked in that the family set up enables the small producer to react more flexibly to outside changes. The ability to draw upon family labour certainly makes it easier to cope with the ups and downs in production. This is vital in branches where instability is a major characteristic of small-scale operations. Within the confines of small enterprises, the availability of family labour gives an almost immediate ability to increase the workforce without necessarily adding to the maintenance cost of this labour. (In most cases it is the wives who 'pay' because in addition to doing the housework they contribute to the production of marketed goods.) Conversely, the family set up makes it easier for the small producer to survive periods without work; hired labour wants to be paid during idle hours; if the enterprise operates from domestic premises, costs of renting a workshop are spared. The practice of improvisation and the integration of family and business produces a system of organisation and accounting which probably goes against all the canons of management text books, but seems important for their competitiveness.

Indeed Lipton (1980) makes this the central argument in a most recent intervention in the informal sector debate; his paper merits special attention in this section, because it centrally addresses a number of issues which arise in the case studies. Lipton's arguments can be seen as directly opposed to those who suggest that the main problem is internal to the small enterprise (even though they are not presented in this context). He suggests that if the small enterprise is a family undertaking, this is its central advantage, 'if the informal sector ... survives and accumulates, it will be due to the sector's own internal economics' (p.1, emphasis added). These advantages arise from what he calls 'extended fungibility', which is the ability of the 'family enterprise to adapt to changed production conditions by adjusting, not only its production behaviour, but also its consumption and reproduction decisions' (p.2).

While his thesis is derived from the observation of rural experiences, his points are very similar to the findings of our urban case studies; family labour can be shared easily between productive activities (producing and selling), reproductive activities (child rearing, housework) and leisure; money for consumption can be used temporarily for production and vice versa; the premises and means of transportation serve production, reproduction and consumption; 'if the same unit ... plans and implements family and enterprise adaptions, flexibility is easier and cheaper ... families with several members of both sexes and different age groups – and families able to hire labour in at some time and out at others – enjoy the greatest advantage' (p.18).

Lipton's 'fungibility' argument is an important contribution to the debate in that it emphasises that factors internal to the small enterprise can be a source of strength, rather than weakness. He rightly points out that the literature on urban small-scale activities largely ignores 'fungibility'. In our own work we did not focus on the integration of family and business from the outset, but it emerged as an important feature in the course of the research. Our observations largely confirm Lipton's concern, but we also noticed instances of conflict between family and enterprise; for instance, parents complained that with increased schooling children showed decreased interest in the business (not reported in the case studies themselves). We can only speculate on whether these attempts to get out of the family business were also linked with the desire to escape authoritarian family structures. Certainly these and other internal problems[12] arising from the close integration of family and business require more attention than a mere mentioning that family enterprises 'are often conflict-ridden, crisis prone or dictatorial' (Lipton, p.81) and also more detailed empirical research than they were given in our work.

In further research on the relative strength of family enterprises, it would probably be important to distinguish between phases of survival and expansion. That 'fungibility' is important to keep small enterprises in business has been emphasised above and can hardly be questioned. As noted by Scott (1979) who also stresses the frequent use of family labour in small-scale production, 'petty enterprises ... survive beyond the point where capitalist ones would have disappeared' (p.122). But is there a point where the integration of family and business becomes an obstacle to expansion?

The relevance of the question is brought out by Lipton's opinion that 'book-keeping and managerial advice seeking to ... separate family from enterprise transactions is unsound' (p.14). This is certainly correct as long as the business relies primarily on the labour of the owner and his family. However, with the increasing use of outside wage labour and the difficulty of supervising this labour there comes a threshold where the non-separation of business and family becomes an obstacle. The supervisory capacity of the family is limited and once paid employees are brought in to act as supervisors, there is a need to formalise organisational procedures and the mode of management. It would be surprising if research on this question did not show cases in which enterprises fail to pass this threshold. After all, it is rarely possible for <u>all</u> small enterprises to grow and (to the extent that factors external to the enterprise allow for expansion) it is likely that those which succeed in growing are those which are well managed. However, this obvious or almost tautological point would neither justify managerial training as the main policy prescription for small enterprises,[13] nor can it justify conclusions that the lack of managerial ability is the general retarding factor in the development of small enterprises. Lipton's argument that the internal factors are a source of strength seems to be more convincing. Even though in certain cases internal factors can work against the expansion of small producers, a restricted form of 'fungibility' can even be expected once the growth of the enterprise has begun to outpace the size of the family.

External Factors

Lipton's emphasis on the internal strength of small enterprises is partly provoked by that part of the informal sector debate which takes a very gloomy view of the development potential of small-scale activities due to <u>external</u> obstacles. He admits that what he calls the 'marginalisation approach' may make sense in some urban activities, but finds that it

- is overconcerned with dependence and exploitation and overstresses the helplessness of small producers,

- as a general theory of non-farm small-scale production is too aggregative and general, giving too little weight to particular technology and market conditions,

- and is 'above all too gloomy' (p.28).

His position culminates in the provocative slogan that 'micro can beat macro' (p.43). The view in the literature which Lipton argues against has been discussed and amply quoted in Part 1 and needs no repetition here. Let us re-examine the issues in the light of the case study findings.

Exploitation

The problem with the issue of exploitation of small producers by larger firms is not so much that it is overstressed; in many studies it is understressed or ignored. The main problem is that it is generally dealt with in a cursory way and rarely substantiated, which is probably linked to the fact that it is both conceptually and empirically difficult to deal with. The case studies underline both the urgency and difficulty of the question, especially in those instances where the family labour is not fully counted in the determination of prices. Are these producers hence exploited? The following remarks cannot solve the issue but suggest a number of points which should be considered in the discussion.

As was stated in Part 1, if the use of poorly remunerated labour (e.g. family workers, apprentices) is forced upon the small producers by other more efficient producers, such labour merely helps to offset the lower labour productivity. Only where their efficiency is not lagging behind does the question of an exploitative relationship between the small producers and the buyers of their products arise. In such a situation exploitation could be said to exist if the return received is less than the equivalent of the number of hours worked, multiplied by the going wage rate in the branch. While this formulation might take us a step further, there remains the question of how to consider the fact that the family workers involved often do not have the alternative of going out to earn elsewhere the going wage rate.

If we ignore this 'complication' for a moment and assume that the return received is equal to or bigger than the above said amount, an exploitative relationship could still arise because an adequate return on the capital invested has to be accounted for. This presents a problem because the capital invested in the workshop is not capital in the general sense, that is, it is hardly transferable to investment in other enterprises but has to be applied in a way which allows the valorisation of the labour of the owner and his family. Thus any idea of 'opportunity costs' of capital is difficult to apply, unless it is in the limited sense of putting the money into a private savings account.[14] Furthermore, certain parts of capital serve not only for production but also for day to day living.[15]

The main point is that in the world of small enterprises the markets for capital and labour are not separate and independent. The allocation of capital is not an abstract choice between freely available alternatives, and the opportunity to valorise labour is linked to a particular application of that capital, since the family workers cannot always go out to work elsewhere (as pointed out already). Given that neither the family's capital nor labour forms part of the general capital and labour markets but makes for segmented markets, it is difficult to put a value on the labour and capital which goes into what the small enterprise produces; hence the difficulty in defining exploitation for such producers.

At the same time there is a need to pursue this question in order to assess whether or to what extent the family enterprise can retain the surplus produced. It is for this reason that the question is pertinent to our study. While the precise degree of surplus extraction is difficult to determine from our case material (not least because of the problems raised above), the structure of the three branches investigated permits some conclusions about the likelihood of such extraction taking place. A producer's ability to retain the surplus is determined by the strength or weakness of his position in the market. In this respect, all three case studies showed the small enterprises as being in an unfavourable situation. They produced under conditions of severe competition (from other small producers), whereas the position of the buyers of their products (generally medium or large-sized enterprises) tended towards an oligopsony. These differences in the degree of competition meant that the small producers had little room to manoeuvre and that the bargaining power lay with medium or large-sized firms. Under such conditions one can expect that a good part of the surplus is channelled away from the small-scale sector, especially if the relationship between small and larger enterprises merges into one of subcontracting. The subcontracting arrangement often ties the small producers to particular firms. As was observed in the case studies, what drives the small producers into this relationship is not just a lack of marketing outlets, but even more the problem of access to working capital or raw material.

In order to give at least an indication of the extent to which the surplus can or cannot be retained by a small subcontractor, his earnings can be compared with those of an independent producer (provided they work under otherwise equal conditions). In the case of the hammock industry we were able to make such a comparison which showed that the independent producer earned roughly twice as much as the subcontracted producer. This would suggest that the surplus syphoned off was indeed substantial.[16]

Nevertheless we shall argue later that the main problem of subcontracting is not so much exploitation (in the sense discussed above) but irregularity of work.

Technology, Markets and Raw Materials

In Part 1 we discussed those contributions to the literature which emphasise that the accumulation prospects of small producers are hampered by technological discontinuities, control of large firms over product markets and access to raw materials. In the case studies these barriers also emerged but to varying degrees. Let us briefly recall the case study findings on these questions, beginning with technology.

The case of the knitting and clothing industry provides a good example of an industry where gradual technological upgrading is possible. In the sewing part of the production process this is so because the dominant unit of production continues to be one operator per machine despite the constant improvement of the machines. In the knitting process there is the possibility of moving from hand operated to mechanised and then to automated machines,[17] but the transition is less gradual than in sewing since the number of machines which can be

171

operated by one person increases with the more sophisticated models.

This is much more pronounced in the weaving industry where the number of looms which can be operated by one weaver has rapidly increased, making it extremely difficult to set up as a small producer. The ability of existing producers to modernise depends considerably on the availability of cheaper second-hand machinery. In most cases the use of such machinery still means lagging behind the most modern technology, but it provides a possibility of catching up a good part of the way. Thus, even though weaving has become a relatively capital-intensive industry, the discontinuities can be reduced through the use of second-hand machinery. Government policies, however, discriminate against the use of second-hand machinery, a topic which will be discussed in greater detail later.

In the case of hammock production we concluded that the likelihood of mechanisation is more limited, and that the technological conditions for the survival and expansion of small producers are favourable. The virtually complete absence of big capital is conspicuous in this case, given the size of the market. The explanation for this cannot be found simply in the lack of scale economies in this industry, but may have to be sought in problems of supervision and control of labour in the work place. It was argued in the case study that where the labour process cannot be controlled to some extent through the machines themselves, large firms tend not to get involved in production itself and leave the field to smaller firms. Big capital could of course try to control the branch through the marketing side, but there was no indication of this in the hammock branch. However, Ayata (1979) shows the preference for big capital to concentrate on marketing rather than production in a fascinating study on the Turkish carpet industry, where the technological conditions are similar to the hammock industry. These ideas need further study and thought, but suggest that the aspect of control and supervision in the labour process be included in an investigation of big versus small enterprises.

The main point arising from the examination of technological conditions is that the discontinuities are not very severe. This is certainly true in terms of available technologies, but to some extent also in relation to applied technologies. The latter is probably linked to a factor which has not yet been discussed explicitly, namely the proximity of the producers to machinery manufacturers or suppliers. We are not sure about its relative importance, but bring it into the discussion because it may contribute to our understanding of why producers are confronted with the technological gap (discussed earlier in section 1.1) in some branches and places more than in others.

The proximity of small producers to technology suppliers was most conspicuous in the case of Petrópolis, because the firm that manufactures the knitting machines is also located in the town. The exact connection between this manufacturer and the growth of the knitting industry is difficult to determine.[18] It seems worth remembering, however, that its range of machines corresponds very well with the technological needs of knitting firms at the different stages in their growth process. The sewing machines (industrial versions) are for the most part imported, but in terms of technological appropriateness this was of no consequence, since the technical change that came in from abroad was of a kind that did not fundamentally affect small-scale production.

In the case of the hammock industry, all the manually operated equipment was produced locally, generally by carpenters. For the few mechanised operations, equipment was 'imported' from the state of São Paulo (which is 3000 km away by road). The lack of interest on the part of machinery manufacturers from São Paulo or abroad certainly meant that the hammock producers were not confronted suddenly with a new technology, but the continued reliance on local manufacturers had the opposite effect in this case: technological progress was extremely limited. This was possibly because making the old equipment was largely a carpenter's job, whereas mechanisation would have required experience in mechanical engineering which is little developed in this region of Brazil but concentrated in the Centre South.

The Brazilian manufacturers of weaving machinery are all located in the state of São Paulo, where Americana is

173

located. Is this why the state of São Paulo has a larger share of small weaving firms and more of a continuum of enterprises of all sizes? To establish such a link is particularly difficult in the weaving industry because it is complicated further by the use of second-hand machinery. Nevertheless, it seems plausible to suggest that the proximity of the loom manufacturers gave the users of second-hand machinery a greater chance of obtaining spare parts quickly. In cases where spare parts were no longer available from the manufacturers, they could fall back on a number of second-hand dealers or small engineering firms which could repair or copy a part. In other words, the existence of a well developed integrated structure in the supply of technology is probably an important context for the growth of small enterprises.[19] Our own empirical work did not sufficiently pursue this connection. If it is of crucial importance, the case studies have probably been conceived too narrowly, a question which will be taken up in the section on research methods.

As regards the product markets in which the small-scale producers operated, they were not as residual as often alleged. Certainly the hammock industry supplied a huge market in terms of number of consumers, even though the size of this market was limited by the low income of many consumers. This was also true for the clothing industry but the characteristic which was of special relevance to its small producers was the unpredictability of the market due to the influence of seasons, fashions and a very diffuse distribution network. Small firms found it easier to cope with the enormous flexibility that was required in such production.[20]

These two case studies provide examples of branches where neither market nor technology characteristics stand in the way of small firms' survival or expansion. Thus they tend to support Lipton's point, mentioned earlier, that it is easy to underestimate the existence of technology and market conditions which favour (or at least do not discriminate against) small-scale production. Above all the case studies underline the need for a differentiated branch-specific approach; for example, even within the textile sector there are vast differences in production and marketing of synthetic fibres, cotton yarn, woven cloth, knitted cloth, garments and hammocks.

One should, however, hesitate in using the case studies to suggest that in Brazil small-scale producers are more likely to escape the macro pressures. In relation to technology it is certainly important that, on the one hand, Brazil has gone further than most developing countries in building up a capital goods industry; this could help to reduce the tecnological gap confronted by small producers in the sense discussed above. On the other hand further research would have to show to what extent the building up of this capital goods industry represents a break from the general tendency in the development of new techniques: the tendency is for research and development to go into improving capital-intensive rather than labour-intensive techniques, as a result of which cost cutting advantages generally benefit large-scale more than small-scale production.[21] According to our information, most of the textile machinery produced in Brazil is copied from machines developed in the advanced industrial countries,[22] even though the degree of dependence on foreign know-how varies in each stage of the production process.

As regards macro pressures arising in marketing, one must assume that they are strong in Brazil. Take for instance improving communications which give distributional advantages to branded, standardised products, especially through advertising. The consequent displacement effects on small producers are acknowledged by Lipton (1980) and studied in detail by Langdon in the study quoted earlier on the Kenyan soap industry. We are not aware of a similar study on Brazil, which investigates the impact on small producers, but in certain product lines it must be powerful since Brazil's television network is rapidly expanding nationwide and relies heavily on income from advertising.[23]

Even if technological and marketing conditions are favourable for small producers, their accumulation prospects can be limited by other constraints. This came out clearly in the hammock case study which showed that problems of access to raw materials can have a crippling effect on the small producers. In this case the price of and access to raw materials had become increasingly unstable through the actions of a large textile company and as a result of government policies, the combination of which seriously threatened the hammock producers. Interestingly Lipton refers to other studies which show 'the periodic non-availability of raw materials', 'temporary shut-downs for want of anything to work upon' and 'workshops are more vulnerable ... since they ... have no ability to carry buffer stocks' (p.32). These findings are very similar to those of the hammock case study and cannot simply be dismissed stating that 'part of the home can function part-time as a store of variable capacity' (p.32), 'labour can be applied domestically if shortages of raw materials briefly choke off its use' in petty commodity production (p.33).

It was agreed before that the family set up can enable an enterprise to survive periods of instability, but Lipton seems to overstate his case when he suggests that the internal advantages arising from 'fungibility' can compensate for the difficulties arising from macro-circumstances of the type observed. Especially when the small enterprise tries to expand and makes investments in buildings or equipment which require periodic repayment, problems in access to raw materials can quickly lead to closures.[24] Again the distinction between phases of surviving (or continuing at the same level of output) and expanding shows its importance for the discussion.

The Role of the State

There is little hope that the state in Brazil would significantly reduce the macro-constraints. Even though the Brazilian Government pledges support for small enterprises,[25] supports where it matters is insufficient or not forthcoming. Why? The main reasons seem to lie in ignorance about the small-scale sector and in its lack of political strength.

The first problem is that so little is known about the small-scale producers. As has been repeatedly pointed out, official statistics tend to substantially underestimate their numbers, and studies about their potential or problems are very rare. This ignorance is of course not simply a result of the complacency of planners, statisticians and researchers who find it easier to deal with a handful of large enterprises than with a multitude of small producers.

The underlying problem is the lack of political pressure which has a number of components: those small producers who are not registered tend to keep a low profile rather than draw attention to their existence, knowing that they stand little chance of successfully challenging the laws or regulations which render their activities illegal. Local governments often reinforce the regulations irrespective of whether this leads to the destruction of small-scale enterprises. When these enterprises are in competition with large registered firms, the latter can even try to do away with this competition by demanding that local authorities take action. An example of this was observed in the knitting and clothing industry of Juiz de Fora, state of Minas Gerais; there the bigger firms launched a campaign to denounce and boycott the small clandestine manufacturers in order to put a halt to the competition which they though disloyal.[26]

Even if the question of registration did not arise, there would still be the problem of small producers actually joining ranks and forming an association in order to articulate their problems and translate them into political pressure. The impression gained in the interviews is that they are generally so involved in the pursuit of their own business, trying to make ends meet, that any form of sustained joint action is unlikely to succeed, even though many think it is desirable. The few cases in which programmes in support of small-scale producers are attempted (e.g. Cabral de Andrade, 1978) are due less to pressure from below than to initiative from individuals (in government, planning or research institutions) who believe in the importance of small-scale enterprises for local economic growth and creation of employment. But even such cases are rare and the programmes are very small.

In contrast, large firms make their needs felt either through the federations to which they belong or by individually seeking direct access to the state.[27] Despite the conflicts that exist between companies, they enjoy wide ranging benefits, many of which are institutionalised.

In fact, the whole incentive structure is geared towards large companies (Cipolla, 1979). This is most conspicuous in the Government's industrialisation programme for the North East. It offers considerable financial and fiscal incentives for investment in the region, for which small enterprises can never qualify because the amount requested for their projects would be too small and because they do not have the required juridical form of business organisation.[28] Furthermore the regulations systematically discriminate against the use of second-hand machinery and encourage the use of capital-intensive technologies, both of which tend to make accumulative growth of local small-scale industry more difficult. The projects which are approved not only have limited direct employment effects, but, more importantly, have few linkages within the region and do little for the creation of new local firms or the modernisation and expansion of existing ones.

The general mechanics of this policy and its effects are amply documented (Goodman, 1972; Goodman and Cavalcanti, 1974; Oliveira and Reichstuhl, 1973; Maus, 1979; Ferreira, Duarte and Soares, 1979). They became blatantly apparent in the hammock industry in three different instances. First, as already noted, a project to set up a new hammock factory would hardly qualify for incentives from SUDENE, since capital requirements would be too small given the labour intensity of production. A second instance was found in the interior of the state of Paraíba where one of the leading hammock producers wanted to build a spinning mill to transform locally produced cotton into yarn for local hammock production; however, he was unable to raise the necessary capital because, given his limited resources, he wanted to venture a mill equipped with second-hand machinery (which is technically and economically a sound undertaking, depending of course on the careful selection of such machinery).[29] Third, as explained before, a large textile company from the South of Brazil managed to gain increasing control of the supply of yarn to the hammock industry; it had been able to occupy this position due to the Government's incentive policy. This had the indirect effect of aggravating the instability in the yarn supply, which hits the small hammock producers in a particularly devastating way. If the Government were to intervene to secure a more stable access to raw materials this company could easily undermine any such attempt, if this were to run against its interests.

All this goes to suggest that the expansion of small-scale industry is indeed hampered by current government policies, as stressed in the recent literature. However, it also suggests that a change of direction is not very probable, because this policy is an outcome of the well entrenched access to the state machinery which large-scale capital maintains.

3.3 Some Policy Implications

It is difficult to believe that policy makers are not aware that the Government's policies work against small enterprises. Nevertheless advisers (in their own ministries, connected research and planning institutions, or even international organisations) are asked for proposals which could benefit the small producers, but would not fundamentally affect the rules of the game which have been enforced. Thus if such advisers propose that the entire incentive structure be changed, their proposals are unlikely to receive much consideration. If they propose that the small enterprises suffer from lack of skill, entrepreneurship and managerial ability, support is likely to be forthcoming. Indeed, managerial training is the favourite recipe prescribed by the Brazilian Government through the 'Centro Brasileiro de Apoio à Pequena e Média Empresa' (CEBRAE) and its local agencies throughout the country.[30]

It was argued above that the internal factors often seem to be the small enterprises' strong point; some lack of organisational ability can occur when these enterprises attempt to expand, but managerial training hardly deserves the priority it is given.[31] One must assume that the continual reference in the policy discussion to the need for better management serves mainly an ideological function. Emphasis on lack of entrepreneurship or management puts the blame for the failure of small enterprises on the people who run them rather than on the environment in which they operate.

Depending on how hostile this environment is, the serious adviser or advice giving body has to decide whether to withdraw and wait for the pursued economic model to crumble or to use the available room to manœuvre. At whatever stage they get involved, policies which aim to give appropriate support to small enterprises must concentrate this support on the branches where the small producers have the possibility of expansion or at least survival. This would apply irrespective of whether the envisaged policies favour producer cooperatives or individual enterprise efforts. Hence it seems necessary to make studies by branch of activity[32] which look at: the technological tendencies in the branch, the pressures which the small producer suffers in competition, in obtaining raw materials, in subcontracting and those which come from legislation or government policies.[33] Only by answering these questions can one arrive at a conclusion about the potential of the branch and possible strangulation points for the small producers. It was partly in response to these questions that the case studies were carried out. Let us therefore consider some of the policy implications which emerged.

In an examination of whether and how to support small-scale enterprises in the weaving industry, the overriding factor is technological change. Increasing scale economies and capital intensity are limiting the entry of new producers and threatening the survival of many of those already established (except in a few lines where the old technology is still viable). Since the superiority of the new technology lies in real cost advantages, this is an example of a branch where a programme designed to keep the multitude of small weaving sheds afloat would be ill-advised. A few small producers, however, might be willing and able to modernise provided relatively up-to-date but second-hand machinery were available. The availability of such machinery is reduced because of the government policy of 'compensatory scrapping'. This rule obliges textile firms which receive incentives and exemptions from import duties to scrap the old machinery.[34] Apparently this policy has frequently led to the destruction of machinery which while no longer the optimal solution for the specific objectives of the investing firm was technically and economically adequate for other usually smaller firms and indeed very much sought after.[35] Thus the removal of this rule combined with halting discrimination in the provision of financial support for the purchase of second-hand machinery would improve the viability of small-scale weaving firms.[36]

The other major problem faced by small producers in this branch, as well as in the other two, was that of instability. This was particularly severe for those involved in subcontracting, since it puts them in a special relationship vis-à-vis market fluctuations. Subcontractors take the brunt of the fluctuations, because their production is the first to be cut in slack periods. Obviously under these circumstances, subcontracting can hardly give the small producer a solid base from which to expand, and its suitability as a measure for promoting small enterprises must be questioned. Judging from the case studies, this instability is the major argument against subcontracting rather than the commonly emphasised exploitation by large firms, which was discussed earlier.

Defenders of subcontracting argue that this would bring about a transference of technology and know-how from the large to the small producers. As mentioned before, Watanabe (1978), on the basis of the Japanese experience, suggests that the subcontractor's productivity can be raised through technical assistance provided by the parent firm, for example advice on how to improve production methods or provision of equipment. In the branches investigated the subcontractors did not receive such assistance, which would anyway require much more steady relationships between large and small firms. These were not given and the 'Japanese model' of large firms playing the role of 'foster parents' of the small ones did not apply.[37]

Access to raw material turned out to be a major stumbling block. This was documented most clearly in the case of the hammock producers. In the knitting and clothing industry the problem also arose but was less striking, probably because a much wider variety of yarns was used, preventing dependence on particular suppliers. In the weaving industry the raw material question as such did not emerge, as practically all small producers are subcontracted and hence supplied by the parent firms. However, what forces the small producer into this relationship is precisely his inability to obtain a regular supply of raw material. This difficulty arises in the first instance out of a shortage of working capital. Indeed, access to working capital was an obstacle in all three branches. However, providing easier access to credit would only solve part of the problem. Direct access to raw material would still be difficult because of the small size of orders; yarn suppliers often have minimum quotas or discriminate in other ways against small customers. Hence small producers rely on middlemen which puts them at a disadvantage costwise. When the middlemen are producers as well, there is an increased risk of being left without raw material, especially in times of relative shortages.

In the case of the hammock industry, the most viable and logical answer would be the setting up of a raw material deposit with a double function: to guarantee access to yarn and to provide working capital. The formula to achieve these two objectives is very simple: the deposit would provide the small producer with the yarn and allow three months for payment. Elsewhere we have made a detailed proposal for such a deposit (Schmitz, 1979b). This proposal emphasised the very low cost per job (created or maintained) of such a project, in comparison to the costs of employment generation in the textile projects aided by the Government through SUDENE. The technical feasibility of a raw material deposit should not be problematic in the hammock branch because the number of different yarn types required is relatively small. The marketing is more difficult to support and administer, but in a second stage, once the deposit is working well, the producers could be brought together in an association which could open up more distant markets for them. The ultimate aim would be a cooperative which would deal with everything from the buying of the yarn to the selling of the finished product.

Such schemes would be much more difficult to

implement in the knitting and clothing industry, due to the enormous product differentiation. A raw material deposit for this branch would have to stock a multitude of different yarn types and colours; a cooperative would be very difficult to run because the number and type of products demanded differ daily and the speed between delivering and ordering is of great importance. (One is reminded of the respondent who said that organising all the small producers would only work if they were to produce military uniforms.) In a branch with these characteristics the policy advisor might therefore 'retreat' to devising a credit scheme even though this would leave the problems of access to lower-priced raw material and marketing outlets unresolved. A more comprehensive scheme along cooperative lines might seem more desirable at first sight, but it could easily undermine the flexibility on which the competitiveness of the small producers is based.

One reason for discussing such proposals is to emphasise the need to derive policy schemes from branch-specific knowledge, if these are to have any chance of succeeding. At the same time one must realise that isolated programmes for a few branches only, if they are not part of a wider policy,[38] can have the effect of provoking a rush into these branches, intensifying competition even further. More importantly, the more the economic obstacles to small producers are entrenched in the macro context, the greater the political obstacles are likely to be to changing the conditions. We have raised this question before, but it is worth reiterating that policy recommendations must be backed by the necessary political power, if they are to be more than pious exhortations.

By way of concluding this section, we should draw attention to a part of the workforce which would probably not be reached, even if the above mentioned schemes were implemented. A programme of support to small enterprises would principally benefit small producers and their families. To a certain extent it would help their non-family workforce as well, since work would become more stable; but there is no reason to hope that the producers would raise the wages of this section of the labour force. In terms of remuneration, the worst off seem to be the women who do the finishing of hammocks at home, whether for large or small enterprises.

The biggest obstacles to the raising of these women's income are their large numbers and lack of work alternatives, which allow the producers to keep payment so low. On the other hand, their large numbers could be to their advantage and strength, if they were united in a union organisation. In fact, this would be the only way of increasing their bargaining power and income.

However, a realistic look at unionisation in the North East of Brazil shows that even the workers employed inside the hammock factories, or in fact enterprises of any other industry, have no union strength whatsoever, the direct result of government policy which suppressed any attempt to establish autonomous labour unions. So the possibilities for the homeworkers to organise themselves must be considered very slim. To suggest that the Government take the initiative and organise this workforce would be a very ambiguous proposal, because the last forty years of Brazilian labour history have shown that the unions, created from the top downwards, became an instrument of containment and control rather than an organisation for the defence or the advance of the rights of the workers.

3.4 Issues of Research Methodology

In this final section the advantages and disadvantages of the research approach adopted in this work will be discussed and contrasted with other approaches used in the recent debate on small-scale production in developing countries. We chose to deal with these methodological questions in detail after presenting the findings, rather than, as one might expect, before in order to make the contrast more real.

Cross-Section Surveys

The manner in which a research project is set up is of course, in the first instance, determined by the questions to be answered and existing information. The world of small-scale producers is in most cases an uncharted territory. They tend to escape official establishment surveys, hence very little is known even about such basic variables as type of activity or number of workers. Cross-section surveys are a useful way of filling this gap and of identifying other characteristics of these enterprises. Indeed, cross-section surveys in selected cities are the most widely used method in the recent research on small-scale activities.

A problem arises when this survey material is used to assess the development potential of these activities. Yet it is precisely this objective which is explicit in many such surveys. For instance, the World Employment Programme of the ILO, one of the main sponsors of research in this field, recommended these cross-section surveys and designed a questionnaire in which 'the main emphasis was placed on the identification of factors that restrict the employment potential and earnings of participants in the informal sector' (Sethuraman, 1976, p.79). The studies which followed the recommended procedure (e.g. Moir, 1978; Fapohunda, 1978; Berlinck, Bovo and Cintra, 1977) provided a good deal of descriptive information, but fell down badly on the question of growth potential or constraints.[39]

The first problem lies in the scope of many surveys which cover small-scale activities of such different nature as manufacturing, construction, repairs, shop keeping, streetselling, bar keeping, taxi driving, and shoe shining. Surely these activities are placed very differently in the economy and are subject to different types of constraints. Even if they have in common the fact that they are neglected or harrassed by the government (as suggested by e.g. ILO, 1972 and Weeks, 1975), this is hardly sufficient reason for analysing them together.[40]

This problem was further compounded by the practice in other studies of identifying the informal sector in terms of persons rather than enterprises (e.g. PREALC, 1978a, Part 1, Chapter 2, and Part II, Chapters 1-4). Again, these studies provide background information hitherto unavailable on the population composing the informal sector, but cannot reveal much on the question of potential, which is raised as a central issue in these studies.

One of the reasons for these problems seems to be that the question of potential and constraints is not separated from the question of poverty and income distribution. Thus concern with the latter leads in many cross-section surveys to the inclusion of virtually all poorly remunerated people, in some cases even domestic servants and casual labourers of large enterprises. This makes the data of little use when the question of potential is examined.[41]

However, even if the unit of analysis is the enterprise and the data are analysed for more narrowly defined groups of activities, the conclusions which can be drawn from these cross-section surveys are limited. Since they aim at statistically generalisable answers, they have to work with pre-set questions and coded answers, which typically lead to findings of the following nature:

> Around 40 per cent of the units did not experience any improvement in their instal-lation in recent years. Another 34 per cent reported only a small improvement. Only 23 per cent reported a significant improvement. (Berlinck, Bovo and Cintra, 1977, p.34)

Or to give another example:

> Between 60 and 83 per cent of respondents in the following activities reported the lack of loan facilities as their greatest problems: food, textile, leather, wood and cork, and furniture manufacturing and construction. Of those in tailoring, repair services and retail trade about 50 per cent regarded lack of loans as a major problem. For manual transport operators and glass manufacturers lack of clients was a more pressing problem.... (Fowler, 1978, p.28)

Similar data are often gathered on age of enterprise or income of its owner, all of which can be useful to make comparisons between the activities covered (e.g. House,

1978), but findings which show that one group of activities fares better on these indicators than others are hardly sufficient to judge complex issues such as the growth potential.[42]

The realisation that survey questionnaires are too clumsy an instrument to come to grips with this issue led some researchers to complement their cross-section surveys with case studies based on discussions with selected producers (e.g. Bose, 1978; Marga Institute, 1978; PREALC, 1978a, Part IV). Significantly it is these case studies which provide the better insights. The reasons are clear: the problems of the small producers tend to derive from a constellation of interlinked factors. This context is more likely to be detected in a freely held (though preferably structured) interview than through a questionnaire in which it is 'chopped up' into separate items. The other reason is a simple and practical one; the respondent is likely to be much more relaxed and forthcoming in a conversation-like interview. This is of particular relevance in research on small-scale producers who are often not registered and therefore need to be reassured that the information is not to be used for purposes of government inspection.[43]

Branch-Specific Studies

Ultimately there is a need to assess the 'view from below', as expressed by the small producers, against information from other sources. The more the constraints they are up against are external to their enterprises, the greater the necessity to subject this external context to direct research. In concrete terms this requires investigating questions such as the respective technological tendencies, the raw material supply, functioning of the product market or government regulations. Data from the small producers themselves are necessary but rarely sufficient. Additional information is needed from technology suppliers (producers of new machinery, dealers in second-hand machinery, repair shops), firms which supply the raw materials (producers of these materials or intermediaries), large firms which compete with or subcontract small firms, and so on.

Once the research has been opened up in this way, it becomes preferable to carry it out on a branch by branch[44] basis for two interrelated reasons: first, factors such as type of technology or markets vary from branch to branch, at least this is an assumption on which the researcher should proceed;[45] second, focussing on a branch enables the researcher to form a whole out of the information stemming from such different sources and thus to 'get a grip' on the circumstances which determine the small producer's potential to accumulate and to generate employment and income.[46]

In summary, if the objective of the research is to understand these circumstances, it seems sensible to delimit the field of study along the same lines as those of the real world, i.e. according to branches and not according to academic concepts such as the informal sector.[47] What is of concern to the small-scale weavers are the actions of the larger weaving firms, not what the small shoemakers or streetsellers do.[48] Cross-section surveys of small-scale enterprises can help to identify those branches in which their numbers are significant; they can help to identify some other basic variables such as number of workers, age of enterprise, legal status and so on; however, they should not be expected to reveal the growth opportunities or constraints of small producers.[49]

Understanding the working of a branch is not just a function of the number of enterprises covered, but also of the way the information is collected. In our own fieldwork we tried to conceive of the producers interviewed (small and large) not just as 'sources of data' but also as 'informants on what is going on in the industry' (compare Peattie, 1978). Thus, apart from collecting information specific to their own enterprise, we discussed their views on the functioning of the branch in general. This procedure proved particularly useful when adopted with respondents who were not producers themselves, but had key positions in the industry, for example, suppliers of machinery or raw materials. Especially in situations where for practical reasons the size of the sample has to be kept small,[50] or where the sampling universe is unknown, this method is of great help. Above all, it acts to a certain extent as a safeguard against totally unrepresentative findings.

The question of representativeness is obviously the major problem in the case study approach. In research in which the field of study is delimited by both branch and region, as in our case studies, this question arises at two levels: (a) how generalisable are the findings on regional industry X for industry X in the country as a whole? (b) how typical is the situation of small producers in industry X for small producers in other industries? A particular danger lies in the likelihood of researchers selecting those branches in which small producers are important, which in turn are likely to be those branches in which they find room for survival or even expansion; in contrast, those branches in which their numbers have dwindled are more likely to be left out.[51] This is why it is necessary in the end to have a combination of both branch-specific studies and cross-section surveys carried out at regular intervals.

In the absence of surveys which cover all sizes of enterprises and are carried out at intervals, it is a hazardous undertaking to draw firm overall conclusions on the question of growth constraints. For instance, Bienefeld (1975) argues that 'detailed observations of 'informal sector' activities always reveal great vitality, considerable technological developments, and every sign of responsive and adaptable growth, while the larger picture remains one of a seemingly endless perpetuation of the sector and its problems ...' (p.73).

What is implied here is that there is a process of growth and destruction, while the net result is one of stagnation. This question is difficult to deal with if comparable surveys carried out at different times are not available. Within a branch-specific study, one can try to reconstruct the past from interviews, but it is always difficult to retrace in this way what has disappeared, and the respondents are more likely to be those who survived or succeeded in growing.

It is believed that these and the previous considerations apply to research in general on the small-scale sector, and obviously must be borne in mind in evaluating the findings of our case studies.

The Wider Context

Irrespective of whether the branch-specific study can draw on comparative longitudinal data, there is the question of the extent to which an understanding of the structure of branch X is sufficient to understand the accumulation process of the small producers within it. In other words, to what extent does their potential depend on the development of the industrial structure in general? In our case studies this became apparent when we considered the connection between the growth of the small-scale enterprises and the development of a <u>local</u> machinery industry. Let us briefly examine this example and consider the methodological implications.

This connection is rarely made in the recent studies on small-scale production,[52] and indeed bringing it into the analysis is a thorny step to take. It leads into the question of how a country can achieve its own indigenous technological capacity. Following the theory of comparative advantage, technologically less developed countries should import the technology from the more advanced countries. However, the import of such technology has been shown to result in considerable capital outflows (Vaitsos, 1974) and the undermining or forestalling of an indigenous process of learning by doing (Cooper and Maxwell, 1975). In the long run it is the latter effect which is the most damaging because it means that the need to import technology is continuously reproduced.

> Industrialisation means ... step-by-step development of production capability by a steady, slow and patient process of learning by doing. It means much more than just setting up certain production capacities, which if need be, of course, can be imported from abroad. If the broad mass of the population is given a part to play in production and is to receive income via that production, suitable conditions must be created for the integration of the broad masses into the ever more differentiated process of division of labour. To this end it is esential that

basic knowledge of alphabetisation, technology
and organisation be imparted and furthered
systematically. Similarly, the organisational
prerequisites for industrial production must be
created and all involved familiarised with
appropriate organisational know-how. It is
precisely these things which no country can
import, but must accomplish itself. It is
possible to import ideas, certain finished
solutions to problems, which can then be
adapted in every country concerned. But the
adaptive capacity itself must exist or be
systematically built up and developed. (Lemper
quoted from Senghaas, 1978, p.23)

Indeed, the need for developing countries to build up
their own technological capacity is increasingly recognised
as a prerequisite for a more penetrating process of
industrialisation (IDRC, 1978; H. Singer, 1977). Some
researchers point towards the need for systematic but
selective government intervention (e.g. Cooper and
Maxwell, 1975; Erber, 1977), others plead for dissociation
from the international economy.

If the countries of the Third World are really to
develop, it is essential to break away from an
unequally structured international division of
labour and the doctrine of comparative costs;
the costs necessary for building up a coherent
economic structure must be classified - as in
the case of every viable economy -as inevitable
learning costs. They are a burden; but
unwillingness to bear them would only mean
carrying over the present structural defects and
their social consequences into the future
(unemployment, marginality, uncontrollable
population growth, crass inequalities of
incomes, etc.). (Senghaas, 1978, p.22)

What we have to set against this view is the relative
success of some newly industrialising countries (Republic

of Korea, Taiwan) in reducing the problems of underemployment through a process of rapid industrialisation characterised by their far reaching integration into the world economy (e.g. Luedde-Neurath, 1980). However, as suggested by Bienefeld (1980), their ability to sustain the success may well turn out to be crucially dependent on the extent to which they pursue their export strategies in conjunction with a long-term policy which emphasises national externalities and the development of a national technological capacity.

Clearly these wider questions can only be addressed at a level at which the whole national economy is analysed in its historical and international context. The need for a global and historical perspective is further demonstrated by the industrialisation experience of the Latin American countries during the two world wars and the world economic recession. During those years their ties to the central economies were weakest and it seems that this contributed to a more sustained process of local accumulation, even though interpretations of these periods are not always unanimous,[53] and rarely cover the development of small firms.

Final Note

Despite the severe difficulties found in the small producers' struggle for survival or expansion the conclusion from the case studies cannot be that there is a definite barrier beyond which they cannot go. The development of small-scale production is not just an outcome of pressures and constraints but also of opportunity and initiative.[54] Fascination with the former can easily lead to deterministic and gloomy predictions, to the denial of all accumulative prospects and to a theory of marginalisation as the general paradigm of small-scale production in the periphery. Such generalisations, perhaps best typified in Quijano's (1974) conceptualisation of the small producers as the 'marginal pole of the economy', should be rejected. At the same time we cannot return to those positions which see the emergence and expansion of small producers primarily as a question of entrepreneurship. First, because this is not the problem (at least this is what has been argued above), and second because the macro pressures emphasised by those who warn about the dangers of marginalisation are real, but the conditions which determine their pervasiveness vary and must therefore be studied and specified.

Hence the issue is not whether small enterprises have growth and employment potential but under what conditions. This question cannot be answered by a mere listing of factors which favour or work against small producers. Such a list would be relatively easy to make. The task ahead is more difficult as the relative importance of the various factors needs to be established. We have suggested above that this can best be done through branch-specific studies. This however, must not be understood as a retreat to the uniqueness of each case. This would indeed mean capitulation in the face of the complexities of the real world and constitute an abdication from theory rather than a methodological advance. The suggestion is made because the branch constitutes the most immediate context in which the small producers operate, and hence is the forum in which many of the hypotheses which form the general paradigms can be most easily investigated. Of course there are other hypotheses which need to be examined in wider studies, as explained above.

Thus, by way of concluding this work, we should emphasise that ultimately branch-specific studies must be situated in wider investigations which encompass the development in the national and international economy. While this could not be done within this work, it should be said that conversely the feasibility or quality of such wider studies will often depend on the availability of detailed branch-specific studies which include the small-scale producers.

Notes

1   A similar result is reported for the self-employed in trade and services in Brasilia (SINE/DF, 1978), but not confirmed for self-employed in urban areas of Bahia (Carvalho, 1976). Tolosa (1975) suggests that the

preference of self-employed for wage employment varies a great deal between regions in Brazil and that it is inversely related to per capita income of the region.

2   This is confirmed by a study on the Peruvian clothing industry which suggests that the 'majority of informal clothing producers do not represent excess labour which chose a second-best activity in the informal sector' (Reichmuth, 1978, p.147). However, in contrast to our findings, most small producers had not been wage workers in larger enterprises of the same branch, but had 'started their activities in the informal sector' and preferred to stay in it (p.97).

3   Thus, the small subcontractor's workshop could be seen as an extension of the parent firm's factory in which he acts as a worker or supervisor who is paid a 'premium' in boom periods and abandoned in times of recession. The 'premium' would be the difference between what he earns as a subcontractor and could earn as a direct wage worker.

4   In Americana's larger enterprises we estimate a yearly labour turnover of 40 per cent. In the hammock industry we found that approximately half the workforce has a length of service record of less than one year (see section 2.4). For the situation in other industries see Estado de São Paulo (1977), Berlinck, Bovo and Cintra (1977), Ely (1978), and Humphrey (1979).

5   Schmink (1980) uses the same distinction in relation to the behaviour of urban households.

6   King's (1974) study of 'Kenya's informal machine makers', which is based on a small number of very detailed case histories, reveals a more complex mobility pattern in which the process of establishing the small business is interspersed with temporary wage employment.

7   Moser (1977) shows for the case of Colombian market sellers how the mobility question is connected with their stage of life cycle.

8   This is of course only a particular instance of the general feature of social mobility providing an escape route which eases some of the tensions of inequality.

9   It could be argued that detailed technical know-how is not essential for good entrepreneurship. This might be valid in large companies, but certainly not in small firms

where the owner is directly involved in the production process, or at least its supervision.

10   This is not to say that attributes such as greed, ruthlessness or single-mindedness are entirely absent among petty entrepreneurs.

11   Thus experience limited to a small number of de-skilled operations on a production line does not provide sufficient technical preparation for self-employment, but significantly most respondents had received a more varied and comprehensive training.

12   For instance, the woman is often the pivot of the small family business, the success of which may well depend on whether she is willing or able first to play the multiple role of wife, mother, book-keeper, co-worker and general care-taker and second to accept the work load and strain which this generally involves.

13   To be discussed further in section 3.3.

14   The capital and the labour of the family could of course be applied in a different branch, but entry barriers, especially skill requirements, limit the small producer's mobility across branches.

15   This restriction of the concept of capital is of course an essential part of Lipton's 'fungibility'. Indeed he (Lipton, 1980) emphasises that a low return 'on capital can well leave family labour as well rewarded as, it feels, is attainable' and that via fungibility 'the capital (cart, house) can earn extra returns outside direct production' (p.73).

16   In the weaving industry such comparison could not be made, since there were virtually no independent small producers. Presumably the parent firms' gains from subcontracting were relatively smaller, because the small subcontractors generally worked with older equipment (lower labour productivity) whereas in the hammock industry there were hardly any differences.

Reichmuth (1978) makes a similar comparison between independent and subcontracted producers in the Peruvian clothing industry. He emphasises that the evidence is not clear cut, but suggests that on balance 'the terms of exchange for subcontracted products are not unfavourable' (p.140).

17   This refers to the type of knitting in which the small

and medium-sized enterprises of Petrópolis were involved. There are other types of knitting in which very expensive automated circular knitting machines completely dominate.

18   There were knitting firms in the town before knitting machines were produced locally, but the beginning of the main growth period coincided with the establishment of the machinery manufacturing firm. Petrópolis itself has not been its only market, it has also supplied other textile centres of Brazil and exported to other South American countries.

19   The absence of such a structure forces firms to internalise certain costs which are likely to increase the minimum scale of operation. For instance, if maintenance and repair services are not available from nearby specialised workshops, the firm might need to employ a maintenance worker; if spare part suppliers are far away, there is a greater need to stock certain parts. Both probably only become economical above a certain minimum number of machines.

20   In the weaving industry, the question of markets did not arise in the same way, because virtually all small producers were subcontracted by large firms which operated in various markets. There was a tendency to use small subcontractors mainly for lower-quality products, but that arose out of the subcontracting system and cannot be taken as an indicator that small enterprises are generally more geared to low-quality products.

21   This effect, originally pointed out by Hans Singer, is also emphasised by Lipton (1980).

22   This is based on interviews held at the International Textile Machinery Exhibition in São Paulo in 1977 with national and foreign machinery suppliers, and on information provided by the Industrial Development Council in 1979. It is interesting to note that Brazil's textile machinery industry owes its existence not so much to a conscious effort on the part of the Government to build up this industry, but to pressures arising from the balance of payments. In order to stem the increase in the balance of payments deficit, the Government introduced in 1975 a compulsory deposit which made imports almost

prohibitively expensive. In the wake of this measure the textile machinery industry expanded very rapidly; however only 45 per cent is under the control of national capital, according to information from the Industrial Development Council.

23   In this context it is worth mentioning that the major advertisers in Brazil (as measured by the accounts of the principal advertising agencies) are multinational companies (Cardoso, 1973). Evans (1979) points out that in Brazil 'mass advertising is the key to commercial success in an industry like tobacco' (p.136) and that 'the tobacco industry ... is a good example of the connection between reliance on advertising and foreign control' (p.201).

24   The importance of the raw material question is further stressed in the section on policies (3.3).

25   See e.g. República Federativa do Brasil (1974), Secretaria de Planejamento (1977), Conselho Nacional de Política de Emprego (1978).

26   According to information from Líscio Camargo who carried out research in this town, and from Diário Mercantil (1978).

27   Based on conversations with individuals who are in charge of executing the Government's industrial policy.

28   The Government's planning and finance institutions for the region (SUDENE and BNB) run a credit programme for small and medium-sized enterprises, but the resources made available are insignificant and the few enterprises that receive support tend to be among the largest in this group (Wipplinger, 1976). Also the lending practices of banks are more geared towards fixed capital (investment in machines), whereas our case studies show a greater need for loans which can be used as working capital (raw materials).

29   In relation to the small-scale enterprises on which we have focussed in this work, the spinning mill project would be a larger industrial undertaking, but its success would strengthen local industrialisation, improve the raw material supply and thus indirectly benefit the small hammock producers.

30   See e.g. Centro de Assistência Gerencial do Estado do Rio Grande do Sul, 1977; Núcleo de Assistência Gerencial

do Piauí, 1977; Ministério do Trabalho/CEBRAE, 1977.

31   Even if it did, judging from our experience of small enterprises on the one hand and advice giving bodies on the other, it must be difficult for civil servants (generally without branch-specific knowledge) to usefully advise small entrepreneurs on how to run their businesses. However, some of the local agencies of CEBRAE have been trying to gain first-hand knowledge of the problems of small enterprises in their region and have begun to devise policy schemes which are more relevant to the needs of small producers.

32   The reasons why branch-specific studies are preferred to cross-section studies are given in section 3.4.

33   If the research is primarily policy-oriented, it seems advisable that those responsible for carrying out the policies are directly involved in the collection of information, because the experience and knowledge so gained of the reality in small enterprises can never be transmitted in a research report, however detailed it may be.

34   The official justification of the policy is to speed up the modernisation of the textile machinery park and to prevent over-capacity.

35   Discussions on this issue with Marcos Panariello of IPEA are gratefully acknowledged.

36   For a concrete case study on the desirability of second-hand machinery in developing countries, see Cooper and Kaplinsky (1975). While this study concentrates on the problems involved in importing second-hand equipment, most of the criteria suggested for the evaluation of such equipment are also valid for a situation in which the machinery concerned does not need to be imported.

37   There is a transfer of know-how from the large to the small enterprises, to which Watanabe also draws attention, which can not however be regarded as a special feature of subcontracting: the movement discussed earlier of skilled workers who give up wage employment and set up their businesses; conversely it was found that part of the workforce of large firms receives its first training in small firms (see section 2.5).

38   One element of such a wider policy would be a change

in laws or regulations easing registration and subsequent tax payments for small producers. This seems all the more justified, considering that large enterprises have a wide variety of legal means of tax exemption or reduction.

39   The mismatch between research question and approach is also glaring in a study which sets out to challenge the optimistic view underlying ILO and World Bank policies (De Coninck, 1980). The author arrives at gloomy conclusions regarding the growth prospects of small producers, but the data collected in a cross-section survey (while interesting in themselves) do not lend themselves to such judgement.

40   Very appropriately Staley and Morse (1965) emphasise at the beginning of their book 'what this study has to say about small industry as a whole is less important than the discriminating judgements and policies it urges as among different kinds of small industry' (p.2).

41   Also on the question of poverty, data on individuals are of limited use, because poverty can only be meaningfully assessed in the context of the family or household, requiring household surveys. For further discussion of these particular conceptual and statistical problems in research on small-scale activities see Bienefeld and Godfrey (1975).

42   Most of the above limitations are also apparent in surveys on the informal sector in Salvador and Fortaleza (North East Brazil), but at least the authors refrain from making general conclusions about the growth prospects of the small-scale activities (Cavalcanti and Duarte, 1980a, 1980b).

43   Compare Fuenzalida et al. (1975) and Reichmuth (1978, Appendix).

44   Compare IDRC (1976, Chapter 4) for the conceptualisation of the industrial branch as a unit of analysis for research and policy. The importance of branch-specific studies in research on small-scale industry is stressed by Nanjundan et al. (1962, Chapter V).

45   One of the main problems in recent informal sector research is that a priori assumptions concerning the conditions of operation of small enterprises entered the definitions instead of being subjected to empirical research. For an extreme case see Sethuraman's (1976) list

of 'criteria for identifying informal sector enterprises' (p.81).

46   Again, there is a practical point which is obvious but can hardly be overstated: the interviewer needs branch-specific knowledge to interpret or query the information given, otherwise be can easily be 'fobbed off' with a few generalities or false information.   This is particularly relevant in research on business which goes unregistered or is carried out in the twilight zone between legality and illegality.

47   Of course, if as a result of a series of such branch-specific studies one can identify a certain pattern across branches, i.e. a group of enterprises that performs differently, one can proceed to conceptualise this observation and put forward new analytical categories which help to explain this situation.

48   Unless there is an autonomous circuit of small-scale operators, separate from the rest of the economy; but virtually all recent studies show that the small-scale activities are functionally integrated into the general economy.

49   PREALC (1979) suggests a methodology to identify from Industrial Census data those branches in which small-scale enterprises have growth and employment potential, but stresses that if applied it can only provide initial indications for posterior micro-economic studies. In any case Industrial Census data are generally deficient. PREALC applied the methodology to the Mexican Census data of 1975; in evaluating this exercise it has to be borne in mind that e.g. for the textile and clothing industry of Mexico it is estimated that 'only some 40% of the production is officially registered' (México, 1978, p.341).

50   Once the need for branch-specific knowledge <u>on the part of the interviewer</u> is recognised, there are serious limitations to the number of enterprises that can be covered, because such work is difficult to delegate. Probably this is one reason why cross-section surveys based on standardised questionnaires are more frequent than the type of research advocated here.

51   There is a parallel in the recent research on choice of techniques where, as Stewart (1978) points out, case

studies were probably only initiated where there was a prior presumption that a range of techniques did exist.

52 But it is made in the literature on appropriate technology. Schwarz (1980) provides a comprehensive account in which he tries to bring the two together.

53 For the debate on Brazil, see Prado Junior (1970), Baer (1965), Dean (1971) and Baer and Villela (1973). Middleton (1979) points out that the Ecuadorian experience does not support the hypothesis that industrialisation is boosted during periods of least contact with the central economies. His study constitutes a comprehensive attempt to analyse the development of small-scale firms in both an historical and international context; but it is perhaps more illuminating on the difficulties of such a complex task than on the nature and intensity of the connections between changes in the macro context and changes at the level of small enterprises.

54 In these final reflections, the work by Lipton (1980) and the recent critiques of dependency theory by Palma (1978), Godfrey (1980), Bienefeld (1980) and Rodríguez (1980) have been most useful.

APPENDIX: INTERVIEW SCHEDULE

The following schedule served as a guideline for the interviews with small producers. It was not used as a questionnaire, but more as a checklist of topics, whose order varied depending on the flow and direction of the interview. Most of the questions listed refer to information on the respondent's enterprise, but the answers were often used as a starting point for discussing their relevance in the branch in general. The general approach adopted in the fieldwork is discussed in sections 2.1 and 3.4 above.

I.   History of firm

1.   Setting up of business (when? how? why?)
2.   Owner's age, previous job, previous experience in this branch
3.   Main changes since beginning

II. Production

1.   Type of product
2.   Stages of production carried out within the firm
3.   Type and number of machines installed
4.   Output (per week or per month)

III. Market

1.   Clients: percentage of production that goes to:-

1.1 wholesalers
1.2 shops
1.3 informal retailers such as streetsellers or stall-holders in market
1.4 direct to the consumer
1.5 parent firms (in subcontracting system)

2.   How is the marketing done? (describe in detail)
3.   Degree of competition in the market:-

3.1 with other small firms

3.2 with large and medium-sized firms

4. Is competition with other firms over price level, quality or other factors (e.g. fashion, product differentiation)?
5. At which consumer income bracket are the products aimed?

IV. Raw materials

1. Source of raw materials:-

    1.1 synthetic fibre companies
    1.2 spinnning and weaving mills
    1.3 intermediaries (yarn distributor)
    1.4 competing large producers
    1.5 parent firm (in subcontracting)

2. Which state does raw material come from?
3. Dependence on particular suppliers of raw material
4. Difference in price of raw material for small and large firms

V. Machines

1. New, second-hand, reconditioned
2. Bought from whom:-

    2.1 manufacturer?
    2.2 dealer?
    2.3 other producers?

3. How financed?
4. Who carries out maintenance?

VI. Credit

1. Is credit available? (from whom, on what conditions)
2. Has loan been received? (from whom, on what

conditions)

VII. Labour

1. Composition of workforce:-

   1.1 total number of workers
   1.2 number of family members/workers from outside family
   1.3 number of minors
   1.4 number of men/women
   1.5 number of workers by occupation
   1.6 number of workers without signed work card

2. Training

   2.1 Where and how was knowledge/training obtained:-

      - to operate machines?
      - to organise production?
      - to calculate costs?
      - to market products?

   2.2 Who received training as employee in other firm?

      - length of this experience
      - post occupied

   2.3 Who learnt mainly through relations, friends, neighbours?
   2.4 Who learnt mainly on the job?
   2.5 Courses provided by machinery suppliers (length, contents)
   2.6 Role of SENAI
   2.7 Length of training time necessary to reach average productivity (for each stage of production)

3. Turnover

3.1 Length of service of workers
3.2 Labour legislation and FGTS: influence on turnover
3.3 Other reasons for turnover
3.4 Is there much changeover of workers between small firms/between small and large?

4. Number of hours worked per week:-

4.1 family members
4.2 employees (outside family)

5. Do some have another job?
6. Wages (by occupation):-

6.1 remuneration of employees (outside family)
6.2 remuneration of family members (adults/ minors)
6.3 for whom are social security payments made?

7   How does income of head of enterprise compare with wages in larger enterprises?

VIII. Subcontracting

1. Working for whom; number of parent firms
2. Type and size of parent firms
3. Why does the parent firm not do the work in own factory:-

3.1 differences in wages?
3.2 social security payments?
3.3 taxes?
3.4 irregular demand?
3.5 greater efficiency of subcontractor?
3.6 other?

4. Do parent firms supply raw material?
5. Did subcontractor receive loan? (conditions)
6. Who supplied machinery?
7. Does the parent firm provide assistance in:-

7.1 organisation of production (management)?
7.2 operation of machines (training)?
7.3 maintenance of machines?

8. Who decides the conditions of payment?
9. Does subcontractor also pass on some of the work?
(if so, repeat VIII)

IX. Registration

1. Is enterprise registered?
2. Cost of registration?
3. Effectiveness of inspections, controls?

X. Costs and profits

1. Costs of production and profit margins (per unit of output)

	Cr $	Percentages
Raw material		
Labour		
Overheads (machines, electricity, rent, taxes, etc.)		
Costs of production		
Profit margin		
Selling price		

2. Percentage of social security payments and taxes in costs of production

XI. Present and future situation of small firms

1. Estimate the number of small firms in this branch in this town, having up to ten people working
2. Estimate the number of clandestine firms
3. Are there many people starting up/abandoning small enterprises?
4. What sort of people generally start up small firms? (previous jobs)
5. The future of the small firm in this branch
6. What measures should government introduce to help small firms?

BIBLIOGRAPHY

The following abbreviations are used in the Bibliography:

BANDECE Banco do Desenvolvimento do Ceará
BNB   Banco do Nordeste do Brasil
BNDE   Banco Nacional do Desenvolvimento Econômico
CEBRAE   Centro Brasileiro de Apoio à Pequena e Média Empresa
CEBRAP   Centro Brasileiro de Análise e Planejamento
CNRH   Centro Nacional de Resursos Humanos
DIEESE   Departamento Intersindical de Estatística e Estudos Sócio-Econômicos
ECLA   Economic Commision for Latin America
IBGE   Instituto Brasileiro de Geografia e Estatística
IDRC   International Development Research Centre
IDS   Institute of Development Studies
ILO   International Labour Office
IPEA   Instituto de Planejamento Econômico e Social
IPLAN   Instituto de Planejamento
INPES   Instituto de Pesquisas
PREALC   Programa Regional del Empleo para América Latina
SENAI   Serviço Nacional de Aprendizagem Industrial
SINE   Sistema Nacional de Emprego
SUDEC   Superintendência do Desenvolvimento do Estado do Ceará
SUDENE   Superintendência do Desenvolvimento do Nordeste
UNDP   United Nations Development Programme
UNIDO   United Nations Industrial Development Organisation
WEP   World Employment Programme

Alves de Souza, G.A. and I. Carvalho, 1977, 'Condições de Emprego no Estado da Bahia: Possibilidades e Limites de uma Ação do Governo Estadual Orientada para o Chamado "Setor Informal" do Mercado de Trabalho', mimeo, Centro de Recursos Humanos, Universidade Federal da Bahia, Salvador.

Bibliography

Arias, A.R., 1978, 'La Pesquisa de Empleo y Renta en la Región Metropolitana de Fortaleza: Resumen Metodológico y Presentación de los Aspectos Más Relevantes de Su Contenido', Informe Técnico No. 38, UNDP/ILO Human Resources Planning Project, Brasília.

Aryee, G., 1977, 'Small-Scale Manufacturing Activities: Study of the Interrelationships between the Formal and Informal Sectors in Kumasi, Ghana', Working Paper 23, Urbanisation and Employment Programme, WEP 2-19, ILO, Geneva.

Ayata, S., 1979, 'Capitalist Subordination of Household Production: the Carpet Industry of Turkey', Paper presented to the Urban Poverty Study Group of the British Sociological Association/Development Studies Association, London.

Bacha, E.L., 1977, 'Issues and Evidence on Recent Brazilian Economic Growth', World Development, Vol.5, Nos. 1 & 2.

Baer, W, 1965, Industrialisation and Economic Development in Brazil, Richard Irwin, Homewood, Illinois.

Baer, W., and A.V. Villela, 1973, 'Industrial Growth and Industrialisation: Revision in the Stages of Brazil's Economic Development', The Journal of Developing Areas, 7.

BANDECE, 1973, Ceará - Polo Têxtil, Fortaleza.

Bandeira, M., 1975, Cartéis e Desnacionalização, A Experiência Brasileira: 1964-1974, Civilização Brasileira, Rio de Janeiro.

Banerji, R., 1978, 'Small-Scale Production Units in Manufacturing: An International Cross-Section Overview', Weltwirtschaftliches Archiv, Vol.114, No.1.

Bell, R.M., 1972, Changing Technology and Manpower Requirements in the Engineering Industry, A Report on a Study of the Science Policy Research Unit, Sussex University Press in association with the Engineering Industry Training Board.

Bennholdt-Thomsen, V., 1979, 'Marginalität in Latein-amerika, Eine Theoriekritik, Lateinamerika - Analysen und Berichte, 3.

Berlinck, M.T., J.M. Bovo, L.C. Cintra, 1977, 'Development of the Economy of Campinas: The Informal Sector', Working Paper 22, Urbanisation and Employment Programme, WEP 2-19, ILO, Geneva.

Bhalla, A.S. (ed), 1975, Technology and Employment in Industry, A Case Study Approach, ILO, Geneva.

Bienefeld, M.A., 1974, 'The Self-Employed of Urban Tanzania', IDS Discussion Paper 54, University of Sussex.

Bienefeld, M.A., 1975, 'The Informal Sector and Peripheral Capitalism: the Case of Tanzania', IDS Bulletin, Vol.6, No.3.

Bienefeld, M.A., 1980, 'Dependency in the Eighties', IDS Bulletin, Vol.12, No.1.

Bienefeld, M.A. and M. Godfrey, 1975, 'Measuring Unemployment and the Informal Sector', IDS Bulletin, Vol.7, No.3.

Bienefeld, M.A. and M. Godfrey, 1978, 'Surplus Labour and Underdevelopment', IDS Discussion Paper 138, University of Sussex.

Bienefeld, M.A. and H. Schmitz, 1976, 'Capital Accumulation and Employment in the Periphery - A Programme of Research', IDS Discussion Paper 98, University of Sussex.

Birkbeck, C., 1979, 'Garbage Industry and the "Vultures" of Cali, Colombia', in R. Bromley and C. Gerry (eds).

BNB/BNDE/SUDENE, 1977, 'Diagnóstico Setorial da Indústria de Confecções', 4 vols., Preliminary Version, Capelin Associados do Brasil, São Paulo.

Bose, A.N., 1978, Calcutta and Rural Bengal: Small Sector Symbiosis, Minerva Associates, Calcutta.

Braverman, H., 1974, Labor and Monopoly Capital, Monthly Review Press.

Breman, J., 1976, 'A Dualistic Labour System? A Critique of the "Informal Sector" Concept', Economic and Political Weekly, Vol.XI, Nos.48, 49, 50.

Brighton Labour Process Group, 1977, 'The Capitalist Labour Process', Capital and Class, 1.

Bromley, R., 1978a, 'Introduction - The Urban Informal Sector: Why is it worth discussing?', World Development, Vol.6, Nos. 9 & 10.

Bromley, R., 1978b, 'Organisation, Regulation and Exploitation in the so-called "Urban Informal Sector": The Street Traders of Cali, Colombia', World Development, Vol.6, Nos. 9 & 10.

Bromley, R., and C. Gerry (eds), 1979, Casual Work and Poverty in Third World Cities, John Wiley & Sons, Chichester - New York - Brisbane - Toronto.

Brun, O. le, and C. Gerry, 1975, 'Petty Producers and Capitalism', Review of African Political Economy, 3.

Cabral de Andrade, A., 1978, 'Programa de Promoção de Emprego Através do Apoio a Micro-Unidades de Produção e a Cooperativas', mimeo, CNRH, Brasília.

Cain, G.G., 1976, 'The Challenge of Segmented Labour

Market Theories to Orthodox Theory: A Survey', The Journal of Economic Literature, Vol.XIV, No.4.

Calsing, E.F., 1978, 'A Política Salarial no Brasil, Um Estudo do Salário Mínimo', Tese de Mestrado, Instituto Universitário de Pesquisas do Rio de Janeiro.

Cardoso, F.H. 1973, 'Associated-Dependent Development: Theoretical and Practical Implications', in A. Stepan (ed), Authoritarian Brazil - Origins, Policies and Future, Yale University Press, New Haven and London.

Cardoso, F.H. 1974, 'As Tradições do Desenvolvimento - Associado', Estudos CEBRAP, 8.

Cardoso, F.H. 1975, Autoritarismo e Democratização, 2nd edition, Paz e Terra, Rio de Janeiro.

Carvalho, I., 1976, Problemas de Emprego em Areas Urbanas da Bahia, Centro de Recursos Humanos, Universidade Federal da Bahia, Salvador.

Cascudo, L. da C., 1957, Rede-de-Dormir, Uma Pesquisa Etnográfica, Serviço de Documentação, Ministério da Educação e Cultura, Rio de Janeiro.

Cavalcanti, C., 1978, Viabilidade do Setor Informal - A Demanda de Pequenos Serviços no Grande Recife, Instituto Joaquim Nabuco de Pesquisas Sociais, Recife.

Cavalcanti, C. and R. Duarte, 1980a, O Setor Informal de Salvador: Dimensões, Natureza, Significação, SUDENE, Fundação Joaquim Nabuco, Recife.

Cavalcanti, C. and R. Duarte, 1980b, A Procura de Espaço na Economia Urbana: O Setor Informal de Fortaleza, SUDENE, Fundação Joaquim Nabuco, Recife.

Centro de Assistência Gerencial do Estado do Rio Grande do Sul, 1977, 'Projeto de Assistência Gerencial à Microempresas', mimeo, Porto Alegre.

213

Bibliography

Chuta, E. and C. Liedholm, 1979, 'Rural Non-Farm Employment: A Review of the State of the Art', Rural Development Paper 4, Department of Agricultural Economics, Michigan State University.

Cipolla, F.P., 1979, 'Proporções do Capitalismo do Estado no Brasil Pós - 64', Estudos CEBRAP, 25.

CNRH, 1978, 'Crescimento Econômico, Emprego e Renda no Brasil', mimeo, Brasília.

CNRH, 1979, 'Indicadores Sociais, Brasil: 1960-1978', mimeo, Brasília.

Conselho Nacional de Política de Emprego, 1978, 'Ações do Ministério do Trabalho no Campo de Emprego e as Funções do Sistema Nacional de Emprego - SINE', Secretaria de Emprego e Salário do Ministério do Trabalho, Brasília.

Cooper, C. and P. Maxwell, 1975, 'Machinery Suppliers and the Transfer of Technology to Latin America: A View of "Packaging" and "Learning by Doing"', Report to the Division for Scientific Affairs at the Organisation of American States, mimeo, Science Policy Research Unit, University of Sussex.

Cooper, C. and R. Kaplinsky with the collaboration of R. Turner, 1975, 'Second-Hand Equipment in Developing Countries: Jute-Processing Machinery in Kenya', in A.S. Bhalla (ed).

Custódio, O. de C., 1976, 'Manual Básico de Malharia', mimeo, Petrópolis.

Davis, L.E., 'The Coming Crisis for Production Management: Technology and Organisation' in L.E. Davis and J.C. Taylor (eds), Design of Jobs, Penguin, Harmondsworth.

Dean, W., 1971, A Industrialização de São Paulo (1880-

-1945), trans. O.M. Cajado, Difel, São Paulo.

De Coninck, J., 1980, 'Artisans and Petty Producers in Uganda', DPhil Thesis, University of Sussex.

Diário Mercantil, 1978, 'Indústria Pressiona Empresário Clandestino', 24 de Janeiro 1978, and 'Indústrias Vão Boicotar Malharias Clandestinas', 26 de Janeiro 1978, Juiz de Fora.

DIEESE, 1973, 'Nível Alimentar da População Trabalhadora da Cidade de São Paulo', Estudos Sócio-Econômicos 1, São Paulo.

DIEESE, 1974, 'Família Assalariada: Padrão e Custo de Vida', Estudos Sócio-Econômicos 2, São Paulo.

DIEESE, 1975, 'Dez Anos de Política Salarial', Estudos Sócio-Econômicos 3, São Paulo.

DIEESE, 1977, 'Salário Mínimo', Divulgação 2/77, São Paulo.

Dhar, P.N. and H.F. Lydall, 1961, The Role of Small Enterprises in Indian Economic Development, Asia Publishing House, London.

Dobb, M., 1975, Studies in the Development of Capitalism, Routledge & Kegan Paul, London and Henley.

Dore, R.P., 1973, British Factory - Japanese Factory, The Origins of National Diversity in Industrial Relations, George Allen & Unwin, London.

Dore, R.P., 1974, 'The Labour Market and Patterns of Employment in the Wage Sector of LDCs: Implications for the Volume of Employment Generated', World Development, Vol.2, Nos. 4 & 5.

ECLA, 1963, The Textile Industry in Latin America, II. Brazil, United Nations, New York.

Bibliography

ECLA, 1969, 'Survey of Small-Scale Industry in Latin America', in UNIDO, Small-Scale Industry in Latin America, United Nations, New York.

Ely, S.M.R., 1978, A Rotatividade da Mão-de-Obra na Indústria Metal-Mecânica de Porto Alegre - Implicações do Sistema do F.G.T.S., Programa de Pós-Graduação em Administração, Universidade Federal do Rio Grande do Sul, Porto Alegre.

Erber, F.S. 1977, 'Technological Development and State Intervention: A Study of the Brazilian Capital Goods Industy', DPhil Thesis, University of Sussex.

Estado de São Paulo, 1977, 'O desemprego em questão', 12 e 14 de Junho 1977, São Paulo.

Evans, P., 1979, Dependent Development, The Alliance of Multinational, State and Local Capital in Brazil, Princeton University Press, Princeton.

Fapohunda, O.J., 1978, 'The Informal Sector of Lagos: An Inquiry into Urban Poverty and Employment', Working Paper 32, Urbanisation and Employment Programme, WEP 2-19, ILO, Geneva.

Ferreira, J.C., R.S. Duarte, F.A. Soares, 1979, Incentivos Fiscais e a Criação de Empregos no Nordeste, Série População e Emprego 7, SUDENE/CAEN, Fortaleza.

FIDAM, 1971, 'Feira Industrial de Americana, Guia da XI FIDAM', Adonis, Americana.

Fisher, D., 1968, 'A Survey of the Literature on Small-Sized Industrial Undertakings in India', in B.F. Hoselitz, The Role of Small Industry in the Process of Economic Growth, Mouton, The Hague and Paris.

Fowler, D.A., 1978, 'The Informal Sector of Freetown (Sierra Leone)', Working Paper 26, Urbanisation and Employment Programme, WEP 2-19, ILO, Geneva.

Frank, A.G. 1971, Capitalism and Underdevelopment in Latin America, Penguin, Harmondsworth.

Fuenzalida, L.A., 1976, 'Criação Mais Rápida de Emprego e Renda Mediante a Expansão e Modernização de Microempresas (Subsídio para um Programa de Assistência Técnica-Financeira às Microempresas)', Revista Econômica do Nordeste, Vol.7, No.2.

Fuenzalida, L.A., R.A. Oliveira, L.A.A. Coelho, S.A.S. Pereira, 1975, 'As Micro-Empresas no Bairro do Nordeste de Amaralina', Documento de Trabalho 5, Estudos para o Desenvolvimento da Pequena Empresa, Universidade Federal da Bahia, Salvador.

Garcia, N.E., 1978, 'Microindustrias en el Sector Manufacturero de Mexico', Trabajo Ocasional 23, PREALC, Santiago.

Gardiner, J., 1975, 'Women's Domestic Labour', New Left Review, 89.

Gerry, C., 1974, 'Petty Producers and the Urban Economy: A Case Study of Dakar', Working Paper 8, Urbanisation and Employment Programme, WEP 2-19, ILO, Geneva.

Gerry, C., 1978, 'Petty Production and Capitalist Production in Dakar: The Crisis of the Self-Employed', World Development, Vol.6, Nos. 9 & 10.

Gerry, C., 1979, 'Small-Scale Manufacturing and Repairs in Dakar: A Survey of Market Relations within the Urban Economy', in R. Bromley and C. Gerry (eds).

Ghai, D., M. Godfrey and F. Lisk, 1979, Planning for Basic Needs in Kenya, ILO, Geneva.

Godfrey, M., 1980, 'Editorial: Is Dependency Dead?', IDS Bulletin, Vol.12, No.1.

Gonçalves, C.E. do N., 1976, 'A Pequena e Média Empresa

na Estrutura Industrial Brasileira (1949-1970), 2 Vols., Tese de Doutoramento Apresentada ao Instituto de Filosofia e Ciências Humanas da Universidade Estadual de Campinas.

Goodman, D.E., 1972, 'Industrial Development in the Brazilian Northeast: An Interim Assessment of the Tax Credit Scheme of Article 34/18', in R. Roett (ed), Brazil in the Sixties, Vanderbilt University Press, Nashville.

Goodman, D.E. and R. Cavalcanti de Albuquerque, 1974, Incentivos à Industrialização e Desenvolvimento do Nordeste, Relatório de Pesquisa 20, IPEA/INPES, Rio de Janeiro.

Hart, K., 1971, 'Informal Income Opportunities and Urban Employment in Ghana', Paper presented at IDS Conference on Urban Unemployment in Africa, University of Sussex; revised version published in The Journal of Modern African Studies, Vol.11, No.1, 1973.

Heyzer, N. and K. Young, 1980, 'Women and the Working Poor: Towards a Framework of Analysis', Paper presented at IDS Conference 'Women, The Working Poor and the Informal Sector', University of Sussex.

Hope, E., M. Kennedy, A. de Winter, 1976, 'Homeworkers in North London', in D.L. Barker and S. Allen (eds), Dependence and Exploitation in Work and Marriage, Longman, London and New York.

House, W.J. 1978, 'Nairobi's Informal Sector: A Reservoir of Dynamic Entrepreneurs or a Residual Pool of Surplus Labour?', Working Paper 347, Institute for Development Studies, University of Nairobi.

Humphrey, J., 1979, 'Operários da Indústria Auto-mobilística no Brasil: Novas Tendências no Movimento Trabalhista', Estudos CEBRAP 23.

IBGE, Censo Demográfico 1950, 1960, 1970, Rio de Janeiro.

IBGE, Censo Industrial 1950, 1960, 1970, Rio de Janeiro.

IDRC, 1976, Science and Technology Policy Implementation in Less Developed Countries, Methodological Guidelines for the STPI Project, IDRC, Ottawa.

IDRC, 1978, Science and Technology for Development, Main Comparative Report of the STPI Project, IDRC, Ottawa.

ILO, 1972, Employment, Incomes and Equality: A Strategy for Increasing Productive Employment in Kenya, ILO, Geneva.

IPEA, 1978, Brasil: 14 Anos de Revolução, Documento elaborado pelo Instituto de Planejamento Econômico e Social e apresentado ao Conselho de Desenvolvimento Econômico, IPEA/IPLAN, Brasília.

IPEA, 1976, 'Panorama do Setor Têxtil no Brasil', Setor de Indústria, mimeo, Brasília.

Kaplinksy, R., 1979a, 'Inappropriate Products and Techniques: Breakfast Food in Kenya', Review of African Political Economy 14.

Kaplinsky, R., 1979b, 'Microelectronic Related Innovations and DC-LDC Trade in Manufactures: Two Sectoral Studies', Research Proposal, mimeo, IDS, University of Sussex.

Kennedy, P., 1979, 'Workers and Employers in the Sphere of Petty Commodity Production in Accra: Towards Proletarianisation?', Paper presented to the Urban Poverty Study Group of the British Sociological Association/Development Studies Association, London.

Kilby, P., 1969, Industrialisation in an Open Economy:

Nigeria 1945-1966, Cambridge University Press.

King, K., 1974, 'Kenya's Informal Machine-Makers: A Study of Small-Scale Industry in Kenya's Emergent Artisan Society', World Development, Vol.2, Nos. 4 & 5.

King, K., 1975, 'Skill Acquisition in the Informal Sector of an African Economy: The Kenya Case', The Journal of Development Studies, Vol.11, No.2.

King, K., 1979, 'Petty Production in Nairobi: The Social Context of Skill Acquisition and Occupational Differentiation', in R. Bromley and C. Gerry (eds).

Kowarick, L., 1975, Capitalismo e Marginalidade na América Latina, Paz e Terra, Rio de Janeiro.

Kowarick, L, 1977, 'The Logic of Disorder: Capitalist Expansion in the Metropolitan Area of Greater São Paulo', IDS Discussion Paper 102, University of Sussex.

Langdon, S., 1975, 'Multinational Corporations, Taste Transfer and Underdevelopment: A Case Study from Kenya', Review of African Political Economy, 2.

Lenin, V.I., 1977a, 'The Handicraft Census of 1894-95 in Perm Gubernia, and General Problems of "Handicraft" Industry', in Lenin, Collected Works, Vol.2, Lawrence & Wishart, London.

Lenin, V.I., 1977b, 'The Development of Capitalism in Russia', in Lenin, Collected Works, Vol.3, Lawrence & Wishart, London.

Leys, C.,1975, Underdevelopment in Kenya - The Political Economy of Neo-Colonialism, Heinemann, London.

Lipton, M., 1980, 'Family, Fungibility and Formality: Rural Advantages of Informal Nonfarm Enterprises versus the Urban-Formal State', Paper presented at Conference of the International Economic Association,

Mexico City.

Luedde-Neurath, R., 1980, 'Export Orientation in South Korea: How Helpful is Dependency Thinking to its Analysis?', IDS Bulletin, Vol.12, No.1.

Macedo, R.B.M. and M.E. Garcia, 1978, 'Observações sobre a Política Brasileira de Salário Mínimo', Fundação Instituto de Pesquisas Econômicas, Universidade de São Paulo.

McGee, T.G., 1979, 'The Poverty Syndrome: Making out in the Southeast Asian City', in R. Bromley and C. Gerry (eds).

McGee, T.G. and Y.M. Yeung, 1977, Hawkers in Southeast Asian Cities - Planning for the Bazaar Economy, IDRC, Ottawa.

Mackintosh, M., 1975, 'The Late Development Hypothesis versus the Evidence from Senegal', IDS Bulletin, Vol.6, No.3.

Malan, P.S., and R. Bonelli, 1977, 'The Brazilian Economy in the Seventies: Old and New Developments', World Development, Vol.5, Nos. 1 & 2.

Marga Institute, 1978, 'The Informal Sector of Colombo City (Sri Lanka)', Working Paper 30, Urbanisation and Employment Programme, WEP 2-19, ILO, Geneva.

Mars, Z., 1977, 'Small-Scale Industry in Kerala', IDS Discussion Paper 105, University of Sussex.

Martine, G. and J.C.P. Peliano, 1978, Migrantes no Mercado de Trabalho Metropolitano, Estudos para o Planejamento 19, IPEA/IPLAN, Brasília.

Marx, K., 1969, Resultate des unmittelbaren Produktionsprozesses, Verlag Neue Kritik, Frankfurt.

Marx, K., 1970, Capital, Vol. I, Lawrence & Wishart, London.

Marx, K., 1971, Capital, Vol. III, Lawrence & Wishart, London.

Maus, T., 1979, Entwicklungspolitik und Unterentwicklung, Ein Beitrag zum Problem der Steuerbarkeit abhängiger Entwicklungsprozesse am Beispiel Nordostbrasiliens, Anton Hain, Meisenheim.

Mazumdar, D., 1973, 'Labour Supply in Early Industrialization: The Case of the Bombay Textile Industry', Economic History Review, Vol.26.

Mazumdar, D., 1975, 'The Urban Informal Sector', World Bank Staff Working Paper 211, Washington.

Merrick, T.W., 1976, 'Employment and Earnings in the Informal Sector in Brazil: The Case of Belo Horizonte', The Journal of Developing Areas, 10.

Meillassoux, C., 1972, 'From Production to Reproduction', Economy and Society, Vol.1, No.1.

México, 1975, Dirección General del Servicio Público del Empleo, PREALC, PNUD, 'Bases Para una Política de Empleo Hacia el Sector Informal o Marginal Urbano', Secretaria del Trabajo y Previsión Social, Mexico City.

México, 1978, Dirección del Empleo, PREALC, PNUD, 'México: La Pequeña Industria en Una Estrategia de Empleo Productivo', Secretaria del Trabajo y Prevision Social, Mexico City.

Middleton, A., 1979, 'Poverty, Production and Power: The Case of Petty Manufacturing in Ecuador', DPhil Thesis, University of Sussex.

Ministério do Trabalho/CEBRAE, 1977, 'Programa de Treinamento e Assistência às Microempresas', mimeo,

Brasília.

Moir, H., 1978, 'The Jakarta Informal Sector', Working Paper 31, Urbanisation and Employment Programme, WEP 2-19, ILO, Geneva.

Möller, A., 1976, 'Los Vendedores Ambulantes de Lima', mimeo, Göttingen.

Moser, C.O.N., 1977, 'The Dual Economy and Marginality Debate and the Contribution of Micro Analysis: Market Sellers in Bogotá', Development and Change, Vol.8, No.4.

Moser, C.O.N., 1978, 'Informal Sector or Petty Commodity Production: Dualism or Dependence in Urban Development?', World Development, Vol.6, Nos. 9 & 10.

Moser, C.O.N., 1980, 'Women's Work in a Peripheral Economy: The Case of Poor Urban Women in Guayaquil, Ecuador', Paper presented at IDS Conference 'Women, The Working Poor and the Informal Sector', University of Sussex.

Moura, H.A. and Coelho J.O.M., 1975, Migrações para as Grandes Cidades do Nordeste: Intensidade e Características Demográficas, Estudos Econômicos e Sociais 1, BNB, Fortaleza.

Myrdal, G., 1968, Asian Drama, An Inquiry into the Poverty of Nations, Penguin, Harmondsworth.

Nanjundan, S., H.E. Robinson, E. Staley, 1962, Economic Research for Small Industry Development, Stanford Research Institute, Asia Publishing House, Bombay.

Nelson, R.R., T.P. Schultz, R.L. Slighton, 1971, Structural Change in a Developing Economy, Colombia's Problems and Prospects, Princeton University Press, Princeton.

Newfarmer, R., 1979, 'TNC Takeovers in Brazil: The Uneven Distribution of Benefits in the Market for Firms', World Development, Vol.7, No.1.

Nihan, Georges, 1979, 'Le Secteur Non-Structuré - Signification, Aire du Concept et Application Experimentale', Working Paper No.7, Technology and Employment Programme, WEP 2-33, ILO, Geneva.

Nihan, Georges and R. Jourdain, 1978, 'The Modern Informal Sector in Nouakchott', International Labour Review, Vol.117, No.6.

Nihan, Georges, E. Demol, C. Jondoh, 1979, 'The Modern Informal Sector in Lomé', International Labour Review, Vol. 118, No.5.

Núcleo de Assistência Industrial - Paraíba, 1975, 'A Indústria Têxtil de Algodão do Estado da Paraíba', João Pessoa.

Núcleo de Assistência Gerencial do Piauí, 1977, 'Programa de Assistência Gerencial e Treinamento aos Empresários de Microempresas do Estado do Piauí, mimeo, Teresina.

Oliveira, F. de, 1972, 'A Economia Brasileira: Crítica à Razão Dualista, Estudos CEBRAP, 2.

Oliveira, F. de, and H.P. Reichstuhl, 1973, 'Mudanças na Divisão Inter-regional do Trabalho no Brasil', Estudos CEBRAP, 4.

Ozório de Almeida, A.L. 1976, 'Industrial Subcontracting of Low-Skill Service Workers in Brazil', PhD Thesis, Stanford University.

Palma, G., 1978, 'Dependency: A Formal Theory of Underdevelopment or a Methodology for the Analysis of Concrete Situations of Underdevelopment?', World Development, Vol.6, Nos. 7 & 8.

Peattie, L.R., 1975, '"Tertiarization" and Urban Poverty in Latin America', in W.A. Cornelius and F.M. Trueblood (eds), Latin American Urban Research, Vol.5, Sage Publications, Beverley Hills and London.

Peattie, L.R., 1978, 'What is to be Done with the "Informal Sector"? A Case Study of Shoe Manufacturers in Colombia', mimeo, Massachusetts Institute of Technology.

Pfeffermann, G.P. and R. Webb, 1979, 'The Distribution of Income in Brazil', World Bank Staff Working Paper 356, Washington.

Polonordeste, PDRI - Vale do Piranhas, 1979, 'Pequenas Empresas Não-Agricolas', Vol.II, Núcleo de Assistência Industrial - Paraíba, João Pessoa.

Portes, A., 1978, 'The Informal Sector and the World Economy: Notes on the Structure of Subsidised Labour', IDS Bulletin, Vol.9, No.4.

Prado Junior, C., 1970, História Econômica do Brasil, 12th edition, Editora Brasiliense, São Paulo.

Prandi, J.R., 1978, O Trabalhador por Conta Própria Sob o Capital, Símbolo, São Paulo.

PREALC, 1978a, Sector Informal - Funcionamento y Políticas, PREALC, Santiago.

PREALC, 1978b, 'Diferenciales de Remuneraciones y Coexistencia de Estabelecimentos de Distinto Tamaño: México 1965-1975', Documento de Trabajo, Santiago.

PREALC, 1978c, Comercio Informal en una Comuna de Santiago, Investigaciones sobre Empleo 11, PREALC, Santiago.

PREALC, 1979, Acceso a Recursos y Creación de Empleos en la Pequeña Industria Mexicana, Investigaciones

Bibliography

sobre Empleo 17, PREALC, Santiago.

Quijano, A., 1974, 'The Marginal Pole of the Economy and the Marginalised Labour Force', Economy and Society, Vol.3, No.4.

Raczynski, D., 1977, El Sector Informal Urbano: Interrogantes y Controversias, Investigaciones sobre Empleo 3, PREALC, Santiago.

Reichmuth, M., 1978, 'Dualism in Peru: An Investigation into the Interrelationships between Lima's Informal Clothing Industry and the Formal Sector', Thesis Submitted for the Degree of Bachelor of Letters to the Board of the Faculty of Social Studies, University of Oxford.

República Federativa do Brasil, 1974, II Plano Nacional de Desenvolvimento (1975-1979), Brasilia.

Rios, J.A. e Associados, Artesanato e Desenvolvimento, O Caso Cearense, Serviço Social da Indústria/ Confederação Nacional da Indústria (no date, probably 1962).

Rocha, J.B.V., 1979, 'Manufatura de Redes-de-Dormir, Um Estudo de Caso sobre a Evolução das Relações de Produção Capitalistas no Nordeste', Dissertação de Mestrado, Universidade de Brasília.

Rodríguez, E., 1980, 'The Articulation of External and Internal Variables and the Industrial Prospects of Peripheral Societies', IDS Bulletin, Vol.12, No.1.

Sanchez Padron, M., 1975, 'Recruitment and Promotion in Some Mexican Firms', IDS Bulletin, Vol.6, No.3.

Sandmeyer, U., 1976, Wahl der Industriellen Technologie in Entwicklungsländern -Theoretische Grundlagen und Darstellung am Beispiel des Nordostens Brasiliens, Institut für Lateinamerikaforschung und Entwicklungszusammenarbeit an der Hochschule St. Gallen, Band 10, Verlag Rüegger, Diessenhofen.

Schaefer, K., 1976, São Paulo - Urban Development and Employment, ILO, Geneva.

Schmink, M., 1980, 'Women and Urban Industrial Development in Brazil', Paper presented at IDS Conference on 'Women, The Working Poor and the Informal Sector', University of Sussex.

Schmitz, H., 1978, 'Emprego Formal e Informal no Setor de Confecções de Roupas no Brasil 1950-1970', mimeo, UNDP/ILO Human Resources Planning Project, Brasilia.

Schmitz, H., 1979a, 'Divergências nas Estatísticas sobre Emprego na Indústrial Têxtil do Nordeste', mimeo, UNDP/ILO Human Resources Planning Project, Brasília.

Schmitz, H., 1979b, 'Factory and Domestic Employment in Brazil: A Study of the Hammock Industry and its Implications for Employment Theory and Policy', IDS Discussion Paper 146, University of Sussex.

Schmitz, H., 1980, 'Technological Change and Labour Utilisation in a Less Developed Economy, A Study of Four Brazilian Industries and Implications for Employment Theory and Policy', Research Proposal, mimeo, IDS, University of Sussex.

Schmukler, B., 1977, 'Relaciones Actuales de Producción en Industrias Tradicionales Argentinas, Evolución de las Relaciones No Capitalistas', Centro de Estudios de Estado y Sociedad, Estudios Sociales No.6, Buenos Aires.

Schwarz, G., 1980, Mikroindustrialisierung: Handwerk und Angepasste Technologie, Institut für Lateinamerika-forschung und Entwicklungszusammenarbeit an der

Hochschule St. Gallen, Band 20, Verlag Rüegger, Diessenhofen.

Scott, A.M., 1979, 'Who are the Self-Employed?', in R. Bromley and C. Gerry (eds).

Secretaria de Planejamento, 1977, 'Programa de Apoio à Pequena e Média Empresa', Planejamento & Desenvolvimento, Ano 5, No.53.

Senghaas, D., 1978, 'Dissociation and Autocentric Development Policy for the Third World', Economics, Vol.18.

Senghaas-Knobloch, E., 1978, '"Informeller Sektor" und peripherer Kapitalismus - Zur Kritik einer entwicklungspolitischen Konzeption', in H. Elsenhans, Migration und Wirtschaftsentwicklung, Campus Verlag, Frankfurt/New York.

Serra, J., 1978, 'Renda Concentra-se Mais nos Anos 70', Folha de São Paulo, 4 de julho de 1978; also in Suplicy et al., 1978.

Servico Nacional de Aprendizagem Industrial (SENAI), Departamento Regional de São Paulo, 1978, 'Indústrias Têxteis e do Vestuário: Presença no Parque Industrial do Estado de São Paulo', Documento de Trabalho, São Paulo.

Sethuraman, S.V., 1976, 'The Urban Informal Sector: Concept, Measurement and Policy', International Labour Review, Vol.114, No.1.

Shinohara, M., 1968, 'A Survey of the Japanese Literature on Small Industry', in B.F. Hoselitz, The Role of Small Industry in the Process of Economic Growth, Mouton, The Hague and Paris.

Sindicato da Indústria de Fiação e Tecelagem em Geral no Estado de São Paulo, 1976, 'Relação das Empresas

Têxteis do Estado de São Paulo', mimeo, São Paulo.

Sindicato da Indústria de Fiação e Tecelagem em Geral no Estado de São Paulo, 1979, 'Carta Têxtil, Edição Especial', São Paulo.

Singer, H., 1977, Technologies for Basic Needs, ILO, Geneva.

Singer, P., 1977, Economia Política do Trabalho, Hucitec, São Paulo.

SINE/DF, 1978, 'O Trabalhador Ambulante no Comércio e Serviços no Distríto Federal', mimeo, Brasília.

Sit, V.F.S., S.L. Wong, T.S. Kiang, 1979, 'Small Scale Industry in a Laissez-Faire Economy, A Hong Kong Case Study', Occasional Papers and Monographs 30, Centre of Asian Studies, University of Hong Kong.

Souza, P.R., 1979, 'Duas "Funções" da Pequena Produção Mercantil na Acumulação Capitalista em Economias Atrasadas', mimeo, Departamento de Economia e Planejamento Econômico, Universidade Estadual de Campinas.

Souza, P.R., and P.E. Baltar, 1979, 'Salário Mínimo e Taxa de Salários no Brasil', mimeo, Departamento de Economia e Planejamento Econômico, Universidade Estadual de Campinas.

Souza, P.R., and V.E. Tokman, 1976, 'The Informal Urban Sector in Latin America', International Labour Review, Vol.114, No.3.

Staley, E., and R. Morse, 1965, Modern Small Industry for Developing Countries, McGraw-Hill, New York - London - Sydney - Toronto.

Steel, W.F., 1977, Small-Scale Employment and Production in Developing Countries, Evidence from Ghana,

Praeger, New York and London.

Stepanek, J.E., 1960, Managers for Small Industry, An International Study, Stanford Research Institute, The Free Press, Glencoe, Illinois.

Stewart, F., 1978, Technology and Underdevelopment, 2nd edition, Macmillan, London and Basingstoke.

Stretton, A., 1979, 'Instability of Employment among Building Industry Labourers in Manila', in R. Bromley and C. Gerry (eds).

SUDEC, 1973a, As Indústrias do Ceará, mimeo, Fortaleza.

SUDEC, 1973b, Mão-de-obra na Area Metropolitana de Fortaleza, SUDEC, Fortaleza.

SUDENE, 1961, 'Sumário do Programa de Reequipamento da Indústria Têxtil', mimeo, Recife.

SUDENE, 1971, Pesquisa sobre a Indústria Têxtil do Nordeste, SUDENE, Recife.

Suplicy, E.M., et al., 1978, 'Debate: Simonsen Contestado por Economistas', Ensaios de Opinião, Vol.8.

Tavares de Araújo Jr., J., and V.M.C. Pereira, 1976, 'Teares Sem Lançadeira na Indústria Têxtil', in Difusão de Inovações na Indústria Brasileira: Três Estudos de Caso, Monografia 24, IPEA/INPES, Rio de Janeiro.

Tokman, V.E., 1978, 'An Exploration into the Nature of Informal-Formal Sector Relationships', World Development, Vol.6, Nos. 9 & 10.

Tolosa, H.C., 1975, 'Dualismo no Mercado de Trabalho Urbano', Pesquisa e Planejamento Econômico, Vol.5, No.1.

United Nations, 1976, Yearbook of Industrial Statistics,

1974 edition, Vol.I, New York.

UNIDO, 1970, Technical Services for Small-Scale Industries, United Nations, New York.

UNIDO, 1979, World Industry since 1960: Progress and Prospects, Special Issue of the Industrial Development Survey for the Third General Conference of UNIDO, United Nations, New York.

Universidade Estadual de Campinas (UNICAMP), 1976, Cadastro Industrial da Sub-Região de Campinas 1975--1976, Vol.I, Centro Técnico Econômico de Assessoria Empresarial da UNICAMP.

Vaitsos, C.V., 1974, Intercountry Income Distribution and Transnational Enterprises, Oxford University Press.

Versiani, F.R., 1971, 'Technical Change, Equipment Replacement and Labour Absorption: The Case of the Brazilian Textile Industry', PhD Thesis, Vanderbilt University, Nashville.

Viceconti, P.E.V., 1977, 'A Industrialização Brasileira', Projeção - Revista Brasileira de Tributação e Economia, Ano II, No.18.

Vieira, D.T., 1968, Pequenas e Médias Indústrias Têxteis, 3 Vols., Programa Delft, São Paulo.

Villavicencio, J., 1976, 'Sector Informal y Población Marginal', Paper presented et CLACSO-Seminar 'Sector Informal Urbano en America Latina', Caracas.

Visão, 1977, Quem é Quem na Economia Brasileira, Editora Visão, São Paulo.

Watanabe, S., 1970, 'Entrepreneurship in Small Enterprises in Japanese Manufacturing', International Labour Review, Vol.102, No.6.

Watanabe, S., 1971, 'Subcontracting, Industrialisation and Employment Creation, International Labour Review, Vol.104, Nos. 1 & 2.

Watanabe, S., 1978, 'Technological Linkages Between Formal and Informal Sectors of Manufacturing Industry', Working Paper 34, Technology and Employment Programme, WEP 2-22, ILO, Geneva.

Watanabe, S., 1979, 'Technical Cooperation Between Large and Small Firms in the Filipino Automobile Industry', Working Paper 47, Technology and Employment Programme, WEP 2-22, ILO, Geneva.

Webb, R., 1974, 'Income and Employment in the Urban and Traditional Sectors of Peru', mimeo, World Bank, Washington.

Weeks, J., 1973, 'Uneven Sectoral Development and the Role of the State', IDS Bulletin, Vol.5, Nos. 2 & 3.

Weeks, J., 1975, 'Policies for Expanding Employment in the Informal Urban Sector of Developing Economies', International Labour Review, Vol.111, No.1.

Wipplinger, G., 1976, Kleine und Mittlere Industrie-unternehmen in Brasilien, Institut für Iberoamerika-Kunde, Schriftenreihe Band 27, Horst Erdmann Verlag, Tübingen-Basel.

Wolpe, H., 1972, 'Capitalism and Cheap Labour Power in South Africa: From Segregation to Apartheid', Economy and Society, Vol.1, No.4.

Woortman, K., 1980, 'Basic Needs and the Working Class Family in Brazil', mimeo, Brasília.